THE YOUNG
HOCKEY PLAYER

THE YOUNG HOCKEY PLAYER

24

Richard Charlesworth
David Hatt

ANGUS & ROBERTSON PUBLISHERS

Acknowledgements

Geoff Fisher (photographer), *The West Australian, The Sunday Times,* Mrs Jill Penter (typist), Dianne Walsh, Janice Davidson, Marian Aylmore, Frances Charlesworth, Terry Walsh, Craig Davies, John Nettleton, Brian Glencross, Sandy Barblett, Jeremy Gallagher, Graeme Walter, Raelene Brindley, Helen Longson, West Australian Hockey Association.

To Frances and Pam

ANGUS & ROBERTSON PUBLISHERS
London • Sydney • Melbourne • Singapore • Manila

First published by Angus & Robertson Publishers, Australia, 1981

© Richard Charlesworth and David Hatt, 1981

National Library of Australia
Cataloguing-in-publication data

Charlesworth, Richard.
  The young hockey player.
  ISBN 0 207 14247 5

  1. Field hockey. I. Hatt, David, joint
author. II. Title.

796.35'5

Typeset in 10 pt Plantin by Graphicraft Typesetters
Printed in Hong Kong

Contents

Foreword

I am delighted to be able to write a foreword to *The Young Hockey Player*, as I consider it to be a most worthwhile addition to the literature available on hockey today. It is with particular pleasure that I observe the suitability, to both young men and young women players, of the information contained in these pages.

Richard Charlesworth is without question one of Australia's greatest ever players, and a keen, perceptive student of the game. As the present Australian captain, Richard has had many opportunities to view the world hockey scene and learn from that experience. The content of this book is a real testimony to the fact that he has done just that. Richard's record as an all-round sportsman is known worldwide, and young hockey players could not find a more appropriate person to emulate.

Richard's co-author, David Hatt, is a former state representative of Western Australia, and is at present coach of the Western Australian state women's team. David is also a past coach of the Western Australian junior team with many years' coaching experience with young people.

With the combination of their talents *The Young Hockey Player* has taken shape. Not only do I believe this book is of value to young players, but it is of great value to coaches, managers and administrators connected with budding hockey enthusiasts. I give it my unhesitating support.

BRIAN GLENCROSS, 1981
Former Australian Olympic captain;
silver and bronze medallist;
national men's selector;
national women's coach.

Introduction

Hockey is a truly international sport. It is a game which is played in over 80 countries involving all continents of the world. The true impact of hockey can be measured by its continued acceptance as an Olympic sport.

It is the aim of this book to provide a basis of fundamental ideas which young hockey players can use to prepare their future in the game. However, we see no reason why such a book should present *only* fundamental ideas as the young player can only benefit from also being confronted with more difficult challenges once he has mastered the basics. For that reason we make no apologies for the more advanced aspects of hockey we have presented and the thorough coverage of "how" some things should be done. In addition to those young players who may gain from the ideas presented, it is hoped that coaches of beginning players will be assisted in their efforts to make hockey a compelling and rewarding recreation, and many senior players may also benefit.

Hockey is a game which may seem very complex to the newcomer. In fact it can be an exceedingly simple sport, once the basic skills have been recognised and practised to a reasonable level of competence. This book makes an effort to present skills training in a practical way which allows the young player to understand why it is important that they be practised. Champion players need to continuously practise their skills in training situations which closely resemble match conditions. The satisfaction gained from executing practised skills in a game is one of hockey's great rewards.

Modern trends point towards a much closer relationship between men's and women's hockey. There is now little or no significant difference in the rules observed by men and women players. It is a conscious decision in this book to make as little distinction as possible between the ways both sexes approach the game.

A constant theme which will be evident is the need for encouraging the young hockey player to retain his individual approach to what is obviously a team sport. That may seem difficult to achieve. However, it is very important that a player is able to be a disciplined team member and at the same time develop the ability to express a natural flair or talent.

Hockey in the present era is in a constant state of change. New training methods, different positional systems and increased professionalism are challenging conventional ideas. However, for the broad purposes of this presentation the conventional approach to position play will usually be adopted. We also believe that to fit the youngster for this new era of hockey, coaches should be aiming for a great degree of versatility and flexibility in the type of player they produce.

Above all else this publication tries to present its information in a clear and simple fashion. We have placed heavy emphasis on illustrations featuring the authors and top players demonstrating the basic skills of hockey. We believe this simplifies the approach a young player may adopt to learning. Too much instruction too soon can often spoil hockey for a young player. A lifetime of pleasure awaits the young hockey player through this most challenging sport. As a player or coach, hockey offers any person great opportunities at local, state or national levels. We trust that this book may start many young people along the way to personal fulfilment in the game.

1

1 Basic skills - hitting

Most young hockey players like to hit the hockey ball hard and often. This is a happy situation as long as it is realised that the hit mustn't be used to the exclusion of all other methods of moving the ball. The main values of the hit, which provides the best method of moving the ball with greatest speed, lie in:

1 *Passing to a team mate* where circumstances are such that the hit would be more effective than a push, e.g. where the team mate is such a distance away that interception is possible if the ball is not hit hard.

2 *Shooting at goal* where the attacker is balanced and has the necessary time to execute a hard shot, because there will be occasions when it will be only possible to flick or push.

3 *Making a clearance from a defensive situation* where a firm hit relieves the defence and gains territorial advantage.

4 *Set play execution,* e.g. hit out in long corner, 15 metre hit etc.

Like all skills in hockey the execution of the hit can be analysed. From this analysis the player can move to effective practice and from there to refinements such as hitting off the "wrong foot" or disguising the direction of the hit.

The aim in hitting should be to develop speed and accuracy. As will be emphasised throughout this book, speed is a vital factor in modern hockey. This does not just apply to running speed but also to speed of skill execution.

Let us examine the principles involved in the hit shown in photograph 1.

Netherlands player Theodor Doyer is in action at the 1979 World Hockey Tournament in Perth, making a clearing hit against Pakistan. The four features of this action are highlighted as follows:

1 The hands are gripping the top of the stick and are together.

2 The feet are comfortably apart and are to the side of and slightly behind the ball.

3 The body weight is moving forward in a side-on position and weight is transferred from right to left foot just prior to impact.

4 The back is bent slightly so that the head is over the ball with eyes firmly fixed on the ball.

The hit in sequence

Now by looking closely at the technique of one of Australia's all-time great fullbacks, Brian Glencross, the hit may be analysed further.

The features of Brian's action in hitting closely follow those of Doyer. Check the following on the four photographs 2(a)-2(d):

1   At all times Brian's hands firmly grasp the top of the stick and remain together. This prevents one hand from working against the other as they would if apart.

2   Brian approaches the ball from behind and to the side. His transfer of weight from right to left foot is smoothly done because his backswing is shallow and measured. If his backswing was wild and jerky he would be quickly thrown off balance.

2a

2b

2c

2d

3   Brian's head remains over the ball's position until well after impact. To do this he bends his back slightly and keeps his eyes firmly fixed on the ball.

4   Take careful note of Brian's feet positioning. At no stage does he become unbalanced by having his feet too far apart, or too close together. Slightly more than shoulder width apart is a useful general rule.

5   The follow through is perfectly executed. Like the backswing, it is long and shallow and does not offend the sticks rule. Brian's stick flows through in the direction he wants the ball to go.

Practice drills

The subject of our instructional sequence, Brian Glencross, has spent countless hours over many years perfecting his hitting technique. Many different methods can be adopted to develop speed of movement and accuracy in your hitting. When learning to hit the ball, slow everything down and master the techniques which Brian has illustrated. Then you can progress to the types of exercises suggested as follows:

Exercise 1

In photograph 3 Brian Glencross has placed a line of practice balls approximately 25 metres from two targets set about one metre apart. He then proceeds to hit the balls in rapid succession, aiming at the gap between the targets. This is done both from a standing position and on the run.

3

Exercise 2

Erect two targets as in exercise 1. Imagine you are a centre half hitting alternate balls to the left and right wings which are represented by these targets. Hit 25 balls to each target in each training session.

If you are having goal shooting practice place each target just inside the goal post of your practice goal area. Hit 25 balls to each target from a moving position.

Hitting practice should be allied to the game situation faced by the young player. Adapt the hitting exercises to particular positions, for example:

1   If you are a right half practise hitting cross-field to your inside left.

2   If you are a winger practise hitting centres from the left or right side.

3   If you are a left back practise your cross pass to the inside right position.

These exercises can of course be made more realistic by having the striker hit the ball to his team mates who are positioning themselves to receive it. This practice is closely allied to that which occurs in a game, when obviously one's team mates will not be stationary targets.

Advanced skills

Hockey is played at such speed in modern times that players are not always able to be absolutely correct in everything they do. The champion hockey player must often make a quick adjustment in technique to suit the circumstances. In photograph 4 Richard Charlesworth shows how to hit at goal from his position at inside right, off the "wrong" foot.

4

1   Richard is hitting off his right foot which was not recommended earlier. However his weight is still coming forward and he has been to the side of and behind the ball before impact.

2   To adjust to the situation quickly, Richard's hands have moved slightly down the handle of the stick to give him a little more control and enable him to shorten his backswing and thus execute his hit more quickly. Note that his hands are still close together on the stick.

3   The two vital points are that Richard's head is over the ball in a still position, and his back is bent. This gives him the necessary control to execute this difficult skill.

It should be stressed again that this movement and others should be learnt *after* the basic skill has been acquired. The ability to hit off the "wrong" foot; to turn the wrists at point of impact to change the direction of the hit and to alter the height and pace of the hit are all to be done after the necessary training hours have been spent on correct technique.

This chapter is closed by showing young players the style of the world's most accomplished striker of the ball in the late 1970s, Paul Litjens of the Netherlands, who has scored over 200 goals in international hockey. Litjens spends literally hours daily practising his magnificent hitting skills. Photograph 5 shows Litjens in training preparing for the 1979 World Hockey Tournament in Perth. Young players should specially note the intense concentration applied by Litjens in training.

5

1

2 Basic skills - trapping

Introduction
In any game of hockey it soon becomes apparent which players are reliable in trapping the ball. The opposite is also true concerning those who cannot trap. If a team has players who cannot trap a high percentage of balls which come their way, then they continually lose possession of the ball and thereby severely restrict their scoring opportunities. For a team to work hard to gain possession and then lose it because of poor trapping is clearly wasted effort. It is obvious that trapping is one of hockey's most basic and important skills.

Trapping is not stopping
One of the best ways to illustrate the real value of trapping is to clearly differentiate it from stopping. Trapping a hockey ball is something like trapping an animal such as a crayfish or a crab. You have trapped it in order to possess it, then cook it, eat it or sell it. Likewise a hockey ball. You trap it and have a purpose in mind for it, once it is in your possession. To merely stop the ball is *not* enough. That is why the skill is called trapping, because the ball is then held in your care. You may have stopped the ball, but be robbed of it immediately by an opponent. The difference may seem small between trapping and stopping, but it is one of a series of differences which enable a player to be successful or not successful.

Aims in trapping
Perhaps we can isolate the main aims in trapping in two facets:

1   Trap at all times when circumstances allow it, on your flat stick side at a comfortable distance in front of your right foot.

2   Attempt to position yourself so that an immediate movement of body and ball can take place after the trap, i.e., don't be flat-footed.

Both of these facets are obvious in the trapping style of Richard Charlesworth in a match against the Netherlands at the 1979 World Tournament in Perth as shown in photograph 1.

1   Richard is allowing the ball to travel across his body so that he may trap it in front of his right foot on his flat stick side.

2   Richard's weight is evenly distributed and his knees are bent, and he is holding his stick at an angle in order to play the ball onto the ground should it bounce up.

3   The head is over the path of the ball and its movement is fixed in Richard's intent gaze.

An interesting feature is that Richard's opponent in that match, Wouter Leefers of the Netherlands, is already making a sideways movement in order to try to stop Richard from making ground on his flat stick side. He is making no attempt to rush straight at the player about to assume control.

It is most important that young players are shown these basic fundamentals as David Hatt illustrates in photograph 2.

2

3

4

Obviously there are times, especially with defenders, where a semi-stationary position can be adopted for trapping. Observe in photographs 3 and 4 how Brian Glencross and David Hatt show balance and concentration while trapping. Both trap the ball on their flat stick side, adopt a crouching stance and are in position to make a positive movement with or of the ball.

Notice particularly how low Brian's right hand is on his stick, giving him strength over the ball.

Types of trapping

Not all trapping is done in a semi-stationary position as we have shown in the early part of this chapter. Because of the speed of the game much trapping is done on the run. However the basic principles from photograph 1 still hold good in the following types of traps.

Receiving on the run on flat stick side

In photographs 5 and 6 follow how Australian player Marian Aylmore positions herself while moving so that she accepts the ball in the area in front of her right foot. She will trap it in such a fashion as to allow herself to pass or move either way without making time-wasting adjustment movements with stick or body.

5

6

Receiving on the run on the reverse stick side

You will be told constantly in this book of the value of keeping the ball on your flat stick side. However there will obviously be times during a game when it is impossible to be able to trap on your flat. Likewise there will also be occasions when it is advantageous to trap on your reverse.

Trapping on your reverse, especially if you are a left side player, becomes a required skill. Australian left side forward Janice Davidson shows how this technique is executed. Note in photographs 7 and 8 how Janice traps the ball well out in front of her, and she can quickly transfer it to her flat stick with a fast stick movement. Note also how she is well over the ball and her weight is evenly balanced as she moves forward. Her right hand is well down her stick to provide the necessary strength to make the trap.

7

8

Trapping in a side-on position

This is a slightly more advanced skill but left side players should be conscious of its application. It applies when neither a semi-stationary trap nor a reverse side trap is appropriate, as in photograph 9. Richard Charlesworth has accepted the ball with his back to the sideline, which has enabled him to be on his flat stick even though moving sideways. Richard's good footwork to get around the ball and eliminate the need to play on his reverse now enables him to be more effective in his disposal of the ball.

9

Exercises to improve your trapping

1   At training get three or more of your team mates at close range pushing the ball to you in quick succession. Without straightening your posture trap each ball and push accurately back to the player from whom you received the ball. See photograph 10 for an illustration of this exercise.

2   The second exercise is very similar to the first except that the balls are being *hit* at the player practising trapping. Don't forget to make a conscious effort to trap on the flat stick side in such a way as to enable a quick pass away. Your footwork will be most helpful here. In photograph 11 Brian Glencross is trapping balls hit to him by Richard Charlesworth, David Hatt and Craig Davies, and is illustrating the required technique.

3   Try the same exercises but this time trap exclusively on your reverse.

4   Again, use the same format, but this time have another player stand near the player trapping the balls, tackling the trapper every time a ball rolls away after a slight mistrap.

5   Maintain the same format, but adapt the movement so that the player trapping moves from side to side, trapping on the run, both on the flat and reverse sides.

Remember — it is not enough to merely stop a ball. To trap a hockey ball is to accept it and take it into your care. You keep it till you are ready to pass it away when the time is right. Have a purpose in mind every time you trap a ball.

10

11

1

3 Basic skills - pushing

The push represents one of the simplest yet most important facets of the game. Many believe this skill, along with dribbling on the flat stick, should be the first skill any beginning player learns.

The push stroke may not be able to impart the same speed onto the ball as a hit but there are many other advantages to be gained from its frequent use:

1 *To pass disguising intent*
Firstly, a push can be easily disguised — the timing, direction and speed of the ball can be very easily kept hidden from one's opponents. The reason for this is that there is no telltale "back lift" as occurs when one hits the ball. As the stick is not taken away from the ball and as the push is performed with hands apart on the stick, it can therefore be undertaken while dribbling or after stopping the ball without the opponents having time to anticipate a pass.

2 *To enable quick disposal* (i.e. quick pass, quick shot at goal)
Because the push allows us this opportunity to pass, shoot at goal or clear the ball quickly it is an essential part of the repertoire of every hockey player. Junior players (and indeed many senior players) tend to use the hit too much and thus their game may lack subtlety because the opposition is able to anticipate their passes.

3 *Set play execution*
Not only is the push an essential part of field play, it is a very important aspect of a number of the set plays in hockey (see chapter 7). The push in from the side line, the penalty corner and the penalty stroke all require a player to have mastered the stroke. Likewise many free hits anywhere in the field may be taken with the correct execution of a push.

Photograph 1 illustrates the push shot as executed by Australia's hockey captain, Richard Charlesworth, in a league match in Perth. Note:

1 Back bent, knees flexed.

2 Hands apart.

3 Eyes on ball even after ball has gone.

4 Follow through!

Points to remember
Using a sequential photographic series we can now break down the push stroke into its component parts. Refer to photographs 2(a)-2(d) on page 24.

1 The player stands *to the side and behind* the ball. The player is *side-on* and generally his left shoulder is pointing in the direction of his intended stroke.
   Naturally this is the ideal starting position, however you will learn that during a game one often finds it necessary to push from a less than perfect position (i.e. the ball may be behind, directly in front or even on the reverse side).

2a

2b

2c

2d

2   The *hands are apart* on the stick. Left hand at the top. Right hand approximately halfway down. You will realise that this is the same hand positioning that is used for trapping and dribbling.

3   The actual push entails two simultaneous movements:
- There is an *explosive action of the right hand forward* in the direction of the ball while the *left hand moves in the opposite direction* (see photo).
- At the same time the body *weight is transferred rapidly* from right leg to being evenly distributed and onto the left leg which has stepped forward to the side of the ball. As the stroke is made the weight continues to be thrown forward as the *stick and body follow through.*

4   Throughout this whole action there are one or two other aspects which bear mentioning. Firstly, at all times the striker keeps his *eyes on the ball* even as it leaves his stick for its destination. Finally it should be remembered that the *back is bent* to some degree at all times and the *knees are flexed* also.

3

4a

4b

4c

Advanced skills

1   Usually the striker's left foot points in the direction the ball is to be pushed (see photograph 3). However this may not necessarily be the case, and indeed, by pointing the foot in one direction and pushing in another, the experienced player can disguise the direction of the pass (photo sequence 4(a)-4(c) demonstrates this technique).

2   The ball need not necessarily be flicked off the left foot. Sometimes, especially when the ball must be pushed from the left side of the field to the right, one pushes off the "wrong" foot (i.e. right foot). This generally occurs when the player doesn't have time to be positioned correctly, wishes to disguise the pass or is running with the ball.

Practice exercises

Perfecting the push shot and its various subtleties requires hours of diligent practice. A few of the standard methods of undertaking this are outlined:

1   Stand in pairs opposite one another. The ball is pushed from one to another with, firstly, a conscious effort to use the correct technique. As the players become more confident and adept, then variations of the direction and pace of the ball can be instituted (photograph 5 illustrates this technique).

    To add interest to this form of practice, a competition can ensue wherein each player makes a "goal" approximately 6-8 metres apart separated by a distance of 15 metres. The players can effectively disguise the speed and direction of their pushes in a competitive situation.

2   For accuracy — shooting at targets — see photos 6(a) and 6(b). The player places two targets approximately 10 metres away to the right and left. Then, using a number of balls, alternately pushes to each target endeavouring to improve accuracy and maybe even on occasions disguise the direction of the pass (note foot position in photograph 6(b)).

A further extension of this practice which can simulate the match situation is if an independent observer calls (at random) the target to which the next push is to be made. In this way the pusher has to make a sudden adjustment and learn to combine speed with accuracy.

5

6a

6b

4   Basic skills – dribbling

Even the uninitiated observer can usually appreciate the skill of dribbling — the ability to run at different speeds with the ball under control. It is certainly one of the most fascinating and spectacular facets of any hockey match. To master the full magnitude of all aspects of dribbling is a very difficult task taking years of dedicated practice by the young aspirant. However, if the task is undertaken in stages it is possible for the young player to make consistent progress.

Traditionally the very finest exponents of dribbling skills came from the Indian subcontinent (India and Pakistan) but it is now possible to see these skills being demonstrated by players in many top hockey playing nations. The fluent movement of such players while changing speed and direction should be observed by the young player whenever possible, as watching champion players is one of the best ways to learn.

Finally it must be stressed that dribbling takes place not for the sake of "looking good" but it serves a purpose for the team. If used when necessary and combined with good passing skills, dribbling can be the spring board to many goals!

Dribbling skills can be useful in the following situations:

1   To out-manoeuvre the opposition so that a pass can be used to eliminate them.

2   To "beat an opponent" in a man to man situation when combined with a feint or body swerve.

3   To carry the ball with safety and moderate speed — obviously the passed (hit or pushed) ball travels faster. However dribbling often represents the safest way to get the ball into position for a shot at goal or to clear out of defence if a team mate isn't immediately available to receive a pass in an uncontested position.

4   To enable the team to maintain possession of the ball when combined with passing movements.

The simplest aspects of dribbling will be looked at first, before progressing to more difficult and challenging facets.

Dribble on the flat stick side
This is one of the simplest skills to learn yet if perfected it can be devastatingly effective when allied to speed, ability to "feint" and "swerve" and change pace and direction. Much emphasis is often given to the so-called "Indian dribble" which is described later, but it is felt that this skill is of equivalent importance as it allows the player to move with greater speed and less chance of error.

Photograph 1 (page 28) gives a perfect study of a player dribbling on the flat stick side. Pakistan's inside right, Mansoor Hussain Jun., is captured in action against New Zealand in the Esanda Hockey Tournament (Perth, 1979).

Points to note on the photograph on page 28:

1   *Bent back* (as emphasised elsewhere, this is important in many hockey skills). With the ball kept in front of the body, the player is still able to "scan" from this position, enabling him to see what is going on around him.

2   *Hands apart* (as for trapping and pushing). The right hand is approximately halfway down the stick — the left hand is at the top.

3   *Eyes on the ball* (at that *instant* but as you will see later it is also necessary to look around while dribbling).

4   *Ball in front and slightly to the right of the right foot.*

2

The young hockey player can usually dribble on the flat from the outset provided the playing surface is reasonably smooth. Assuming the correct position, the ball is propelled ahead with a tapping motion of the stick so the ball is just a few centimetres in front of the stick. With increasing confidence the ball can be cushioned on the stick's surface throughout the whole exercise.

Photograph 2 shows a young player practising his dribbling skills. He is fortunate to be able to practise on the "perfect" Astroturf surface at the Commonwealth Hockey Stadium in Perth.

A position of strength
Having the ball on the right or flat stick side is to have it in a position of strength. The player with the ball on his flat can invariably brush off any reverse stick challenge. There are few occasions in hockey when it is advantageous to have the ball on one's reverse rather than flat stick side.

In photograph 3 Australia's right half, David Bell, has the ball and he intends keeping it on his flat stick side. Two Canadians are endeavouring in vain to wrest the ball from David's control. They are both using their reversed sticks!

3

The Indian dribble

This method of dribbling is a logical progression from dribbling on the flat and its mastery allows the young player to increase his repertoire substantially. By perfecting the Indian dribble a player becomes able to pass or change direction to the left or right without giving notice of his intent. Thus the young player can then move on to the more complex skills of eliminating an opponent by change of direction, selling dummies and body and stick feints.

In the Indian dribble the ball is played alternately from the flat stick side to the reverse stick side as the player runs with the *ball in front of his body*. It can be simply considered a flat stick dribble in which the player regularly plays the ball to the reverse stick side and back again. This analogy holds true except for the fact that, unlike in the flat stick dribble, the ball should not go far outside the line of the right foot if at all. To perfect this skill at speed with assurance takes much practice.

Starting to Indian dribble

The young player should first learn to play the ball from "flat to reverse" and back while stationary, then once he has mastered that, he can walk and eventually run doing the Indian dribble.

Photographs 4(a)-4(c) demonstrate the Indian dribble while stationary:

1　The ball is played from the line of the right foot to that of the left foot.

2　The position of the right-hand arm is virtually unchanged in each photograph. Clearly the stick has rotated within the grasp of the right hand, which acts as a guide but which only "firms" when the ball is played with flat or reverse.

3　The left hand has rotated approximately 180 degrees. This is clearly visible from the wrist position in 4(a) and 4(c). While the left hand is chiefly responsible for this rotation, it should be noted that the right hand plays a part in initiating this rotation.

With practice the Indian dribble in a straight line is soon mastered. Once this has been accomplished players should then practise their dribbling skills against obstacles. A time-honoured method is to place the obstacles in line and attempt to dribble "in and out" using alternately the flat stick side and then the reverse, in the manner of a slalom skier.

4a　　　　　　　　　　　　　　4b　　　　　　　　　　　　　　4c

5

6a

6b

Photograph 5 shows a group practising slalom using the Indian dribble. Photographs 6(a) and (b) demonstrate the technique used on the reverse and on the flat.

(a) To change direction from flat stick side the player pushes off his right foot to move to his left — the ball is ahead of and well inside the right foot.

(b) To change direction from reverse side the player pushes off his left foot to move to his right — the ball is ahead of and inside the left foot.

7

Application

In photograph 7 the mastery of the Indian dribble allows West Australian state player Sharon Buchanan to retain control of the ball using her reverse stick after she has beaten her opponent.

It will be seen later that the ability to play the ball alternately with flat and reverse sticks (the Indian dribble) is an integral part of being able to beat an opponent whether as an individual or by using a pass.

Speed while dribbling

The faster the player moves with the ball the further the ball is generally played out in front of the body (and the more upright is his position to allow him to run faster).

Photograph 8 shows Richard Charlesworth, who has just come into possession of the ball, accelerate away from an opponent. The ball has been tapped out in front as Charlesworth endeavours to "get going".

Photograph 9 again demonstrates the style of Mansoor Hussain of Pakistan. Here he is moving at top pace and you will note his more upright position and the increased distance at which the ball is being played away from his body.

8

9

10

Passing while dribbling

When a player wishes to pass the ball while dribbling on the flat it is necessary to position the ball to deliver the pass.

1   *To pass left* the ball may be hit or pushed off the "wrong" foot or it can be moved to the line of the left foot and passed. In photograph 10 Richard Charlesworth has moved the ball to his left and is awaiting the right moment to deliver his pass.

2   *To pass right* using the flat stick the player moves the ball further outside his right foot to enable him to scan in that direction and pass when ready.

11

12

13

Photograph 11 illustrates Australia's inside right, Richard Charlesworth, in action during the Esanda World Hockey Tournament in 1979. He has the ball well outside his right foot in preparation to make a pass to his *right* as the Great Britain captain, Bernie Cotton, comes in to tackle him.

One of the advantages of the Indian dribble is that as the ball is generally played in front of the body rather than on the right, it is possible to pass left without making it obvious. Likewise, if the player is able to perfect the reverse stick pass, then the ball can be passed right from the same position in front of the body.

Looking up while dribbling

When dribbling it is vital to know what is going on around you — where are your opponents; team mates; are they moving or stationary; where is the best pass? While running with the ball under control you should become adept at "looking up" or "scanning" in order to make a quick assessment of the situation ahead and then return your gaze to the ball and allow your peripheral vision to deal with the situation you have seen developing. As players ahead are constantly changing their positions, any player travelling any distance with the ball will usually "look up" a number of times. Video film of champion players shows that they look up approximately three to four times every 20 metres they run with the ball!

Photograph 12 demonstrates graphically Australia's captain "looking up" to make an assessment of the situation ahead of him even while hotly pursued by a Great Britain opponent, David Westcott. Charlesworth, even though moving at speed and being contested, still demonstrates the importance of knowing what is ahead. Similarly in photograph 13, Charlesworth has propped and is guarding the ball while taking time to assess the best pass by "looking up".

Practice skills

Any practice should take place in stages — firstly master the dribble at slow speed with correct technique before advancing to more difficult practices at greater speed.

1   Try balancing the ball on your stick for 30 seconds (see photograph 14 on page 38). If you are able to do that then bounce the ball up and down on your stick 30 times. These practices help to get your "eye in" and while simple in concept require good co-ordination of eye, ball and stick. The same co-ordination is necessary for successful dribbling.

2   Simply walk — jog — run in straight line dribbling, firstly on the right then with the Indian dribble.

3   Make two relay teams — compete against one another at speed — see how often you err!

4   Use a line of obstacles and conduct relay races again. Each player has to dribble out and back three times before the team has finished.

5   Now stagger the obstacles as shown in photograph 15 on page 39: this makes the dribble accent the change of direction which you will later realise is so important in "beating an opponent". Try to accelerate for a few paces as you pass one obstacle and head for the next.

6   Place the obstacles in line with a 10 metre space in the middle. Deploy your players to each end; one of them has a ball. The coach or one player is in the middle of the 10 metre gap but a couple of metres off centre.

14

A player dribbles the ball through the obstacles and at the gap passes off to the coach, receives a return pass and continues through the rest of the obstacles. At the end of the line the ball is passed on to the next player who goes in the opposite direction, reaches the gap, passes, receives and eventually gives the ball to another player at the same end as the original dribbler. With two at each end you can do this exercise until fatigued.

7 Finally, it is useful to practise dribbling on the reverse by simply running in a straight line with the ball being propelled with the reversed stick on the left (see photograph 16). While this is discouraged, and we emphasise that the reverse should only be used when absolutely necessary, it can be a useful form of practice. The main benefit lies in the strengthening of the left hand and the gaining of confidence in using the reverse when it is necessary.

15

16

1a

1b

5 Basic skills - tackling

Tackling is a skill which is quite often neglected by young hockey players and their coaches. It tends to be unspectacular in comparison with other actions on a hockey field. However the young player should perhaps reflect on the number of times a tackle has to be made in the course of a normal match, and how important these may be to the team's performance.

The tackling action of a player should be a very thoughtful movement. Hitting and trapping can quite often become almost routine tasks requiring concentration rather than original thought. However, almost every tackling situation will be different and obviously requires a special effort in concentration.

The aims of a tackle

Broadly speaking there are perhaps three aims in making a tackle. They are:

1   To win possession of the ball from an opponent.

2   To spoil an opponent who has control of the ball.

3   To place pressure on an opponent and force a bad pass to be made.

As in previous chapters, the principle is adopted that it is best to show the skills being executed and highlight the outstanding features of this execution.

Firstly however, we should categorise the various types of tackles to be discussed. These are:

1   The lunge tackle

2   The poke tackle

3   The wrong side tackle

The lunge tackle

This tackle is obviously so named because of the lunge by the tackler with the left leg forward and stick extended in the left hand.

There are two examples of this tackle featuring top Australian representative male and female players. In photograph 1(a) Craig Davies is tackling Richard Charlesworth. In photograph 1(b) Dianne Walsh is tackling Marian Aylmore.

As indicated in the photographs, the four outstanding features are:

1   Both Craig and Dianne have adopted virtually side-on positions to make their tackle. The lunge is made with wrist locked to put firmness and control into the tackle.

2   As with other skills, the back and knees are clearly bent. With this tackle it is even more pronounced.

3   The angle of the stick is very low, which gives the tackler maximum coverage of the ball should the attacker suddenly change direction.

4   Craig and Dianne are both intently watching the ball. This principle is vital in tackling. Too many tacklers watch only the opponent's stick or body which may be swerving or feinting attempting to "wrong foot" a defender, or catch the defender off balance.
Note: Should Dianne miss her tackle initially, she is in a position to run quickly back to make another tackle because of her side-on stance.

The poke tackle
Usually this tackle occurs when the player in possession of the ball is not moving quickly and may be holding the ball looking for an opening in a defence. Without fully committing his body, the defender may quickly jab his stick forward and attempt to make the attacker lose control and then win possession or force a free hit. This tackle can realise any one of the three aims we expressed at the beginning of this chapter.

In photograph 2, Craig Davies is tackling fellow international Peter Haselhurst in a match to mark the opening of the Commonwealth Hockey Stadium in 1979. Craig has effectively spoilt Peter's control with his tackle. Note that while Craig is more chest-on to Peter, he is still not fully committing himself to the tackle.

2

Wrong side or reverse side tackle
This tackle is so named because it involves a player tackling an opponent on his non-flat (or reverse) stick side. As a general principle young players should be conscious of the need to tackle as often as possible on their flat stick side with the lunge or poke tackles. The young player should not allow a situation to develop where wrong side tackles are continually being made. However credit must be given to opponents who may force this tackle to be made from time to time.

In the sequential photographs 3a-3c, watch how a Great Britain attacker, Cemlyn Foulkes, has broken away from Australian inside left Mal Poole and forces Australian left half Grant Boyce to make what is a well executed wrong side tackle.

Young players should note the following features of Grant's tackle:

1   At no stage does Grant's gaze shift from the ball as soon as he realises Mal Poole's effort to back-tackle will not succeed.

2   Grant positions himself so that he runs alongside his opponent, waiting for the most effective time to tackle.

3   As Grant makes the tackle his back is bent and he gets to a close in position next to his opponent.

4   As with both the lunge and poke tackles, the reverse stick tackle is made with the left arm extended with the wrist firmly locked.

It is important that young players realise that when making wrong side tackles they are close to their opponent. This avoids the chance of injury which can easily happen by making thoughtless tackles on the wrong side.

3a

3b

3c

An incorrect tackle

It is sometimes easier to explain what not to do when tackling rather than what should be done because the circumstances of a tackle vary so much during a game. In photograph 4 some of the wrong things are rather graphically illustrated. The Indian defender has made an ineffective attempt to tackle Netherlands forward Ron Steens and allowed easy access to the goal circle. The incident took place in the Esanda World Tournament in Perth in 1979. A goal resulted from this movement.

1   The Indian player is chest-on to the defender and has been caught flat-footed.

2   While his back is bent, his eyes are not on the ball and he has over-balanced forwards.

3   By gripping the stick with two hands in this situation the defender has lessened the potential width of his tackle, which is poor use of reach.

4   The three previously mentioned points add up to the fact that the defender has eliminated himself by his action. He will not be able to recover to make a second tackle.

4

The bullfight tackle

Everybody knows the manner in which a bull charges the matador when he waves a red cape. Unfortunately some hockey players act this way by running at full speed to a player with the ball. Because they charge so quickly the player in control of the ball merely pulls the ball aside as a bullfighter withdraws his cape. As with the bull, the hockey player goes roaring past, not having gained possession. Don't run at a player who has full control of the ball. Slow down and think before you commit yourself.

Points to think about when making a tackle

Position yourself as often as possible so you tackle on your flat stick side.

Try to make your opponent make the first move, not yourself. Delay your move until you're confident of success.

Aim to tackle slightly side-on in order that you may quickly retreat if your first move is unsuccessful.

Always be on your toes when making a tackle and be conscious of the need to take small steps to quickly alter direction if it becomes necessary. Try to baulk your opponent into going the way you want.

Photograph 5 shows a thoughtful poke tackle by a Canadian player against Australian Trevor Smith at the 1979 World Hockey Tournament in Perth. The Canadian is well balanced with eyes carefully following the ball, and he can quickly move sideways if Smith changes direction.

5

Suggested exercises to improve your tackling

Running alongside opponent

Ask your training partner to run with the ball attempting to beat you over a 30-40 metre distance. Run alongside your opponent, but do not tackle. Ask your partner to change pace or direction as often as is wished. You should be concentrating on what are the best times to tackle. You may get three or four chances in that 30-40 metre distance. Also note how many times your partner loses control of the ball, kicks it or obstructs you. This should be a good lesson in the wisdom of a delayed tackle.

Repeat the exercise several times and then try it again, but tackle properly and attempt to win the ball.

In photographs 6(a) and (b) Richard Charlesworth and David Hatt demonstrate this exercise, with both a reverse stick and flat stick tackle.

Shadow tackling

Without a partner, and no ball, practise moving quickly from side to side, backwards and forwards, making lunge and poke tackles at imaginary targets. This will be very tiring and may last just a short while before you need to rest.

6a

6b

7a

7b

Tackling opponents in quick succession
At a team training session have four or five of your team mates attempt to dribble around you in a restricted area. As soon as you have finished tackling one, the next should be onto you and so on. This will improve your reflexes and help your concentration for match situations. If you have five team mates attempting to dribble round you (one at a time) they should do this at least four times so you make 20 tackles. You then change over and allow a team mate a turn. Watch this demonstrated in photographs 7(a) and (b).

Tackling is for everyone
The most important message for this chapter has been left until last.

In keeping with our stated intentions in this book we stress that all young players should learn all the skills, not just those traditionally associated with defenders or attackers.

Therefore, whether you are a forward or a defender you must be able to tackle. Too often in senior ranks we see forwards who are incapable of making a thoughtful tackle, and simply run at a defender without any real aim. A game of hockey does not stop for a player when an attack has broken down. It is up to a forward and a beaten defender to run back quickly and tackle or at least try to spoil the opponent's pass.

All players should practise their tackling as hard as they practise any other skill.

1

6   General skills

This chapter is devoted to what may be termed general skills. That is, skills which are not absolutely basic to the game but are nevertheless most important. In some instances these skills are extensions of some already discussed. For example, we can say in general terms that the flick is very closely related to the push as outlined in an earlier chapter.

No hockey player is a complete player without the acquisition of the preceding basic skills and this chapter's general skills do not cover all the refinements which exist in the game of hockey. However, we have decided to include the following five areas which we hope will add a further dimension to your knowledge:

1   The Flick

2   Passing

3   Marking

4   Talking

5   Handstop

The flick
Some people would argue that there is little difference between the flick and the push. This may well be true in some respects but young players should appreciate that the flick has functions which give it individual importance. A flick is designed to lift the ball off the surface so that its height may either eliminate opponents by travelling over their heads or present a difficult goal shot for a goalkeeper to save.

If, for example, a player can find no space between a defence for a push or hit method of passing, a solution *may be* to flick the ball over opponents' heads or sticks into empty space behind them. Care should be taken not to make the flick dangerous by avoiding having the ball land in a crowded area or by endangering other players by flicking too low.

Observe the classic flicking action of Richard Charlesworth during the 1977 Australian Hockey Championships in Perth.

Photograph 1 shows Richard, an inside right, in the process of flicking an overhead pass to his right wing. As shown there are four vital features in the execution of this skill:

1   Richard's right hand is doing the hard work and is responsible for the power of the flick. He has positioned his right hand well down the stick to give himself leverage for the skill.

2   Balance is a key to flicking and Richard is almost stationary. His weight has been firmly transferred onto his left foot at point of impact with the ball, and his right foot acts as a steadying factor.

3   Note that the face of the stick is inclined slightly upwards, as the left hand has brought the top of the stick closer to the body. This gives the ball elevation, but it is worth noting that too much elevation results in the flick being ineffective.

4   Richard's eyes are firmly fixed on the ball, which is placed further in front of the left foot than for a push.

In general terms the flick is similar to the pushing action. The real difference between the two skills is that the ball is placed further in front of the body and the player must reach and get down very low behind the ball, flicking it with the stick slightly inclined upwards.

Note carefully how the skill is performed in sequence by international representative Marian Aylmore in photographs 2, 3 and 4.

As with the push, Marian is to the side of and behind the ball when beginning to flick. It can be seen that Marian appears to be almost reaching for the ball as it is further in front of her left foot than for a push. To help raise the ball note how low Marian bends to ensure that her right hand gains the support of her body weight. She keeps her eye on the ball even when it has clearly left her stick.

It is important that the ball is not flicked too high as this gives opponents time to take position to intercept the pass. The path taken by a flick should be clearing your opponents' heads by about one or two metres.

The overhead flicked pass or flicked shot at goal can be practised in exactly the same manner as the push (see exercises in chapter on pushing). An extremely good illustration of the flicked shot at goal can be seen in the chapter on set plays, where Pakistani forward Kalimullah is seen flicking a penalty stroke in sequence.

Finally, it should be noted that the flick is a very difficult skill to master yet top players are able to perform this skill not only while stationary but also on the move — only with much practice can you also do this.

Passing

Passing has been mentioned both directly and indirectly in this book on many occasions, especially in other skills chapters. Therefore it is not intended to dwell on this skill in isolation. If a person executes a push correctly and accurately then this usually means that an effective pass has been made. The same situation occurs with a hit or flick.

What is perhaps important for young players is to understand the types of passes referred to in hockey:

Flat or square pass
For instance, where a pass is given from an inside left to inside right, or left half to right half and so on, as shown in figure A on page 52.

The ball is given square, not at an angle. It is not intended for ground to be made, simply for possession to be held, direction of play to be changed and opposition defenders to be forced to move.

Through pass
Occurs when a ball is passed through a gap amongst opposition players so that a team mate may run onto the ball. See the basic idea illustrated in figure B on page 52. In figure B, the example given is where the inside right has caught the two defenders, the left back and the left half, square with each other and controls a pass through the gap, allowing the right wing to move behind them and run onto the ball.

2

3

4

Obviously there are many angled variations to these passes. Circumstances in a game obviously dictate that diagonal or straight passes may be given — however the through pass and the square pass are the most commonly referred to in traditional positional hockey.

A. Flat or Square Pass

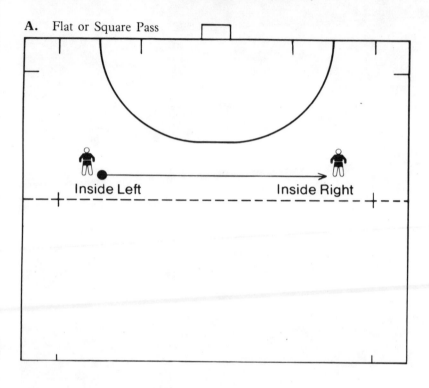

B. Through Pass

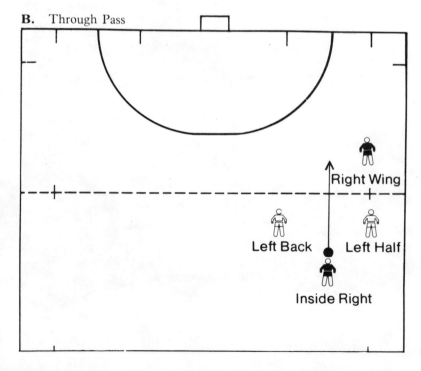

Passing to a team mate's flat stick

Wherever possible young players should aim to pass to the flat stick of a team mate. The reasons for this should be fairly obvious. A ball is easier to trap and control if it is played on the flat stick side. However it is not just the responsibility of the person passing the ball. The player receiving the ball must make every effort to place himself or herself in a position where the ball can be received on the flat stick side. That is, both the passer and the receiver combine to move their bodies and the ball in order that it may be trapped in the most advantageous position.

Marking

The changing nature of hockey in the past decade has meant a real emphasis on the ability of players to "mark" or cover opponents when possession of the ball is lost. Young players should be aware of the fact that it is not enough to stand between their immediate opponent and the ball. With two man offside now firmly established as a rule of the game, correct marking becomes more important as attackers can easily find space behind a defender.

Basically the golden rule in marking is for players to stand between their immediate opponent and the goal they are defending, in such a fashion as to be in a position to trap or tackle on the flat stick side.

Perhaps it would be most advantageous to show what should not be done, and then what should be done.

Photograph 5 shows international Dianne Walsh (light skirt) attempting to mark former West Australian player Frances Charlesworth (dark skirt). However, Frances has been allowed to get behind Dianne and is in a good position to accept a pass from a team mate. Dianne has probably made the mistake of simply watching the ball and not her opponent.

5

6

7

Photographs 6 and 7 show Brian Glencross (light shirt) correctly marking Richard Charlesworth (dark shirt).

In photograph 6 Brian is a left side defender marking a right side attacker. Note that Brian is in a position to cover Richard no matter where he moves and if necessary tackle on his flat stick side. Brian is also in a position to watch the possible flight of the ball.

Photograph 7 shows the same principle but on this occasion Brian is acting as a right side defender marking a left side attacker. Note that in this situation Brian leaves a little more space between himself and Richard.

Young players should be aware that marking requires a continuous mental discipline, and that a team effort requires a defensive and an offensive function to be carried out. Marking is an unspectacular task but a very important one.

Talking

Hockey is a team game where the ball moves at great speed with quick changes of direction. To help players pass accurately, to cover defend and mark correctly, to make maximum use of available time with the ball, and in fact carry out most of the actions of hockey, it is vital that team mates talk to each other continuously. Perhaps young players should consider the following ideas as examples of some of the many types of talking which can and should be encouraged on the hockey field:

A team mate has trapped the ball in the clear and is unaware of this situation. A loud call of "you have time" may help possession to be held or a constructive pass to be given.

A defender may have lost contact with an immediate opponent who has led well for possession. A call of "she's on your right" from a team mate can help to save a goal being scored.

A loose ball in the defensive goal circle may result in hesitation by defenders. A decisive call from a team mate of "yours, Robyn" may save the situation.

Simple encouragement of the nervous or out of form team mate is a responsibility of all players. Even if the talk is "that's good running into position Jenny", a player can gain confidence as a result of being praised.

When a goal is scored don't just praise the scorer — look for all those involved in the build-up.

When a player is in clear space she or he should not hesitate to call for the ball. Whether it is received or not is immaterial — the team mate in possession is at least provided with another alternative. The call should be clear and concise, e.g. "here if you like Bobbie".

Make talking a habit at training sessions. It is a skill which can be the catalyst to a greater realisation of the more practised ball skills. One final point on talk — if you have nothing positive or constructive to say on a hockey field then everybody will benefit by you keeping quiet.

Handstopping

During the course of a game of hockey a ball is bound to be raised either

8

intentionally or accidentally. As the sticks rule can be broken by raising the stick to stop a high ball, the hand must be used instead.

This is well within the rules of the game. The handstop in set plays such as penalty corners is categorised differently and is discussed in the chapter devoted to set plays.

In photograph 8 David Hatt demonstrates the handstop. Observe how the fingers are spread and the hand is slightly cupped to cushion the impact of the ball. Try to ensure the hand is still when the handstop is made. As also shown in photograph 8, the handstop has been made with the left hand. This is recommended wherever practical but it is by no means obligatory.

7   Set plays

Over the past couple of decades set plays have played a large part in determining the results of hockey matches, especially at international level. Increasingly teams have become more and more adept at scoring from corners and penalty corners. Likewise the importance of free hits and push ins close to the scoring circle has become evident — these situations can often bring about the valuable corners and penalty corners.

While this facet of the game is obviously of great importance and a complete chapter is devoted to it, there are certain overriding principles which should be mentioned:

1   At a junior level coaches should encourage their teams to score field goals rather than "set piece" goals as this will afford the young aspirant the best chance of developing as a well rounded and flexible player.

2   Most junior coaches will be aware that set plays are difficult to perfect anyway, as the fields for juniors are often not good and time for such drilling can be better spent at different activities.

3   It is also likely that rule changes in the next 10 years will make set plays of less importance and thus as today's youngsters move into senior ranks, field goals will be their aim anyway.

4   Taking into account the above factors the junior should still realise that the discipline, team work and skill required to carry out these plays are essential to your hockey development and they can only be mastered by assiduous practice.

For the purpose of this chapter the set play situations are divided into two groups:

1   In the field

2   In the circle

In the field
This group of set plays includes all situations where one team has a free pass of the ball in order to get the game going again or where there is a bully, for whatever reason.

Push ins
These occur when the ball crosses "wholly" over the sideline. The team that didn't touch the ball last must place the ball on the sideline, close to the point where the ball crossed the line, and one player must push the ball along the ground while *all* other players are at least five yards (4.5 metres) away.

Obviously these situations can be the source of problems to a defence when they occur close to the scoring circle. The player pushing the ball in should always endeavour to find a team mate and thus allow his team to maintain possession — this will often mean the ball will be pushed back, but this can frequently be done without any danger.

1

Bullies

The bully is only mentioned for the sake of completeness. It is used to start the game, at the beginning of each half and after each goal. Occasionally, for example after an injury stoppage, a so-called "onside bully" will be awarded by the umpire anywhere on the field — on these occasions all players must get in a position such that they are closer to their backline than the ball.

Photograph 1 demonstrates a bully — the players are facing one another on opposite sides of the ball and must touch their sticks over the ball three times before playing it. All other players must be at least five yards (4.5 metres) away.

16 yard (14.6 metre) hits

A 16 yard hit is awarded when the ball crosses the backline after being (*a*) played off an attacker's stick or (*b*) accidentally played off a defender's stick from outside the 25 yard (22.7 metre) line (inside the 25 yard line a corner is awarded).

The defending team can take the "hit" from a position adjacent to where the ball went out and up to 16 yards (14.6 metres) from the backline. Most prefer to use the full 16 yard allowance, but on occasions the hit will be taken closer to the backline.

The obvious aim of any defender taking such a hit is to find a team mate; if this is not possible the next aim should be to make as much territorial advantage as possible while avoiding opposition players.

Free hits

Almost anywhere on the field except in the circle, a free hit is awarded for a breach of the rules — in some cases (corners etc.) a more severe penalty is given.

The advantage of a free hit is that it allows the offended team to get possession and therefore your main aim in taking a free hit should be to maintain possession. The ball may be hit or pushed along the ground and in most cases a team is best served by taking any free hit quickly and continuing to allow the game to flow.

Once again it is obvious that free hits around the circle can be of great advantage to attacking teams and thus time should be spent working out ways of deriving benefit from these occasions.

All of these situations have been dealt with briefly as we believe that they exist merely as ways of getting the game moving after a breach or the ball going out of play. To place too much emphasis on these situations would lead to the development of a very stereotyped and stilted game of hockey.

In the circle

Because of their positioning each of these situations represents a chance to shoot at goal and therefore they are of great importance to any team. Remember, in international competition more than 50 per cent of goals come directly or indirectly from penalty corners or corners.

Penalty (or short) corners

A penalty corner is awarded by the umpire in the following circumstances:

1   Intentional breach by a defender inside the 25 yard (22.7 metre) line.

2   Any breach by a defender inside the circle.

3   Intentional clearance over own backline by a defender.

What happens:

1   The ball is hit or pushed from the backline, five yards (4.5 metres) inside the circle.

2   The attacking team must be outside the circle when the ball is hit or pushed from the backline.

3   Six members of the defending team must stay behind the backline until the ball is hit or pushed into play — the other five must wait at the centre-line.

4   The ball must be stopped (not necessarily motionless) with the stick or hand and the attackers may then shoot at goal.

In photograph 2 on page 60 Charlesworth is positioning himself prior to taking a "push out" for a penalty corner. Note:

1   How low he is getting in preparation to push.

2   He is taking a last minute look at where he will push the ball.

3   The player in the foreground is bending in preparation for making his handstop.

In photograph 3 on page 61 Richard Charlesworth demonstrates his style as he practises a "push out". Note:

1   Eye on ball.

2   Weight transfer forward to follow through.

Note: Some teams prefer to hit the ball out, others to push; while the hit travels out with greater speed the push gives the defenders less chance to anticipate and start running. However the essential feature of either method is accuracy. A fast and accurately delivered ball allows the hitter and

2

handstopper to position themselves correctly and time to shoot without having to hurry and change their footwork.

   Photograph 4 shows Tim Steens of the Netherlands handstopping for Paul Litjens. These two are a part of what is perhaps the best corner battery in the world. Note:

1   Intense concentration by Steens, getting down low to make the handstop — he is wearing a glove.

2   Litjens has already started his backswing and is stepping in to strike the ball.

3   The Dutch player in the foreground is moving into the circle preparing for a possible rebound. He is taking no interest in the handstop and hit — he is preparing for what may eventuate after the hit!

3

4

The attackers

In most grades of hockey the favoured method of scoring off penalty corners is for the push out to be handstopped and the team's most powerful hitter to strike the ball into the goal. The other attackers are deployed around the circle to take advantage of rebounds or any variation which may have been organised. Two players generally have the job of running in on the pads (photograph 5).

In teams with very efficient corner batteries the time lapse from push out to shot at goal is between 1.4-1.8 seconds so it is important that every player knows his job and performs his functions correctly.

Photograph 5 shows England goalkeeper Bob Taylor making a copy book save off a corner shot by New Zealand. Taylor's two team mates are positioned on the posts and another English player is waiting to clear a rebound.

Most important though is the position of No. 14 from New Zealand. He has run in to collect any rebound that might occur off Taylor's pads. This is where good forwards should be!

Photograph 6 depicts former West Australian captain and present coach Richard Aggiss on his "down swing" as handstopper David Bell has just lifted his hand off the ball after making his stop.

Note: Bell is stepping back while Aggiss, with eyes firmly focused on the ball, is leaning into his hit with a very fluent display of hitting style and weight transferral.

The defenders

While ability to score from penalty corners can be vital it should also be remembered that a side's ability to defend them is also vital. Four elements play a part.

1   Fast player to run out and block the initial shot or at least force the attackers to hurry and therefore err. This player generally runs from a position on the goalkeeper's left so as not to obstruct his view.

2   Sound goalkeeping — the goalkeeper usually takes a couple of paces towards the hitter but must be balanced, usually on his toes.

3   Players with the ability to trap shots wide of the goalkeeper on the goal line.

4   Well positioned defenders to clear any rebounds which may fall out of the goalkeeper's reach.

Photograph 7 demonstrates the first three of these points. The Dutch team is attempting to save a powerful shot from India's Surjit Singh in the World Tournament in Perth, 1979.

Corners (or long corners)

A corner is awarded when the ball goes out over the backline having last touched a defender's stick within the 25 yard (22.7 metre) line and the backline — if it last hit a defender's stick outside the 25 then a 16 yard (14.6 metre) hit would be awarded.

What happens:
The displacement of the attackers and defenders is the same as for a penalty corner, viz.

1   Ball hit or pushed (most prefer to hit) from backline or sideline five

5

6

7

8

metres from corner flag on the side of the goal over which the ball went out.

2   Attackers outside circle (until ball into play).

3   Six defenders behind backline, remainder at halfway line.

4   Ball stopped with stick (or hand) and attackers may then shoot at goal.

   Photograph 8 illustrates Richard Charlesworth taking a hit out for a long corner from the point five yards (4.5 metres) from the corner flag.

1   As the ball must be delivered with speed and accuracy and with only a minimum of warning to defenders, the player must hit the ball from a standing position. To develop maximum power and accuracy a weight transfer similar to that of a golfer is employed — note the similarity!

2   Also many players prefer to shorten their backswing to avoid telegraphing their intended stroke — to implement this many start from a position in which their stick is already half to three quarters' way back on the backswing.

The attackers
On true surfaces teams are endeavouring more and more to use a handstop and hit but this is a method that because of the larger distances involved can cause great difficulty. In practice a stick stop is still used most often and the player stopping can either shoot at goal or pass the ball around for others to shoot. While corners are generally considered less dangerous than penalty corners there can be great advantage in any team effectively using and carrying them out.

   Attacking teams should also be wary of an opposition interception and breakaway from any corner or penalty corner and should generally have at least three defenders not immediately involved in the corner defending in case of this eventuality.

The defenders

The same basic four rules apply to corners as for penalty corners except that the runner out may have to reposition himself, and also in the case of a stick stop he must be aware of the possibilities of the stopper passing to another attacker or taking himself on!

Penalty strokes

A penalty stroke is awarded in the following circumstances:

1   Any intentional breach by a member of the defending team inside the defenders' circle.

2   Any *un*intentional breach by a member of the defending team inside the defenders' circle which in the umpire's opinion stopped a probable goal being scored.

What happens:

1   Time off is blown.

2   The ball is placed at a spot seven yards (6.4 metres) from the centre of the goal.

3   The goalkeeper (or another) defends the goal while one attacker is allowed to push or flick the ball at the goal after taking only one step and after the umpire is satisfied both are ready *and* has blown his whistle.

4   The stroker is allowed to take only one pace and the goalkeeper must have his feet on the goal-line and is not allowed to move until the shot has been taken. The goalkeeper can catch or save the ball in any way he chooses and once a save has been made (or a goal scored) the penalty is over. Any save in which the goalkeeper breaches the rules (e.g. "sticks" or back of the stick) results in a penalty goal being awarded.

Photographs 9(a)-9(c) on page 66 depict Pakistan's penalty stroke taker Kalimullah in action during a match in the World Hockey Tourney in Perth. These photographs demonstrate Kalimullah's perfect technique in executing a flick stroke and also his intense concentration as he watches the ball closely throughout. The only difference between this sequence and a push shot is that Kalimullah has positioned his left foot further *behind* the ball (than for a push) thus allowing himself to elevate the stroke to the desired height more easily. The result of this flick was of course a goal!

General philosophy of taking penalty strokes

The following guidelines are important for young stroke takers:

1   You must approach the stroke in a positive frame of mind forgetting the situation of the game or any incidents, and your full concentration should be on scoring the stroke. Remember the goalkeeper is probably more nervous than you.

2   Many believe a low push is safer but you should endeavour in practice to master the skill of flicking in any position, high or low to each side. Only by assiduous practice can you become confident about flicking to all corners of the goal. (Practise flicking at targets in an empty goal — keep a record over a few months and your improvement will surprise you.)

9a

9b

9c

3   Make up your mind where you want to flick and don't change at the last moment. Obviously if you know the goalkeeper has a particular weakness then exploit it.

4   Develop a *fast* flick — even if not perfectly positioned they often go in.

5   Most important of all watch the ball — don't look up too soon to see where it went. Invariably those are the ones you miss and watch sail past the post.

Even the best exponents of this skill in the world have missed, so if you fail once you are in good company. What is important is to believe in yourself next time. There is some merit in rotating the flickers in a junior team as this gives all an opportunity to participate and assures that no one player is under undue pressure.

Photograph 10 shows the Indian goalkeeper making an excellent save off a penalty stroke taken by Canada in the Perth tournament in April 1979. As you can see, the goalkeeper has his stick in his left hand and is handstopping with his right.

10

11

The goalkeeper's job saving penalty strokes is very difficult:

1 Certainly the young goalkeeper should be encouraged not to anticipate but rather attempt to develop his reflexes and thereby advance his goal-keeping skills. Going one way is successfully employed by some goalkeepers but isn't recommended for young players.

2 Probably again the goalkeeper should relax (be balanced), and concentrate intensely on the ball and nothing else. His reflexes will do the rest. As a goalkeeper becomes more experienced he may pick up mannerisms and methods used by flickers that give him some clues.

In photograph 11, again the Indian goalkeeper is shaping up to save a penalty. However, this time Paul Litjens' shot was too strong — the result was a goal.

8   Beating an opponent

In any hockey match it is the aim of each team to get shots at goal and to score from those chances. This can only be achieved by eliminating or beating the opposition so that you are able to get the ball into the most advantageous position. Because of the numerical equality of the teams, any game could theoretically be a stalemate, unless a player somewhere on the field is able to get away from or beat his immediate opponent.

Of course in practice errors are made by all players even without the opposition's good play forcing them to be made. However, our skill in passing and dribbling should allow us to beat opponents or at least force them into error. It is not sufficient to wait for things to happen — you must endeavour to make them happen by your good and skilful play.

"Beating an opponent" can be achieved in many ways but basically refers to the many ways of *creating* and *exploiting* a numerical advantage which eventually enables us to outmanoeuvre the opposition and shoot at goal. Although quite a deal of space will be devoted to beating an opponent in man to man situations it must be stressed that:

The best way to beat an opponent is by passing the ball around or past that opponent.

Photographs 1(a)-(c) on page 70 illustrate the use of a simple triangular passing movement to eliminate an opponent. The player in the light shirt is drawn to make a tackle and the ball is quickly passed by the player in possession to his team mate. The team mate almost immediately returns the ball to the near player who has quickly run past his opponent to complete the *triangle*. It should be noted here that the near player had an alternative move available to him. He could have shaped as though to pass to his team mate as in photograph 1(a) and suddenly changed direction and moved to his left, thus beating the player in the light shirt who was anticipating a pass and indeed may have already moved to his left to intercept it. This is known as "dummying" or "feinting" a pass.

There are many ways in which this and other passing movements can be used but they have as their basic prerequisite a numerical advantage on the part of one team. Good teams work on creating situations such as the one demonstrated in order to eliminate opposition defenders. It can be applied when there are two against one or six against five. When such a situation is created or evolves, in any hockey match, it must be exploited.

Beating an opponent in a man to man situation

Many skills and techniques have been demonstrated so far in this book but none require the expertise that is necessary to beat an opponent and *retain* possession of the ball so that you are still able to do something useful with it.

The ingredients required are:

1   *Sound dribbling skills.* (This includes both dribbling on the flat stick and Indian dribble.)

2   *Ability to look up or scan* while dribbling and see what is ahead of you.

1a

1b

1c

3   *Ability to change direction and change speed* while retaining possession of the ball in a dribble. *Correct balance* is an essential part of this.

4   *Perfect timing* — to move too soon or too late is fatal but generally it is true that it is better to move too soon because at least your opponent cannot interfere with your control. Should your move be made too soon and your opponent counters, you are always able to change again and thus beat him. However if you get too close then your opponent will tackle or you may run into him.

5   *Ability to feint (or dummy) and swerve* — a feint or dummy is a movement or action which is undertaken in order to mislead your opponent and which doesn't produce the result he expects or anticipates. A player initiates a particular movement but does not carry it through and then performs a contradictory action which the opposition isn't expecting. The player with the ball has the advantage of knowing *what* he or she is going to do and *when* he or she will do it. Thus the player performs a dummy or feint to mislead the opponent as to his true intention. Once the opponent has responded to the dummy (by moving to tackle) the player then performs the contradictory action for which the opponent is unprepared.

In many situations it is necessary to outwit your opponent by such actions and they can be particularly effective in enabling you to beat an opponent in man to man situations.

Feinting and swerving
There are basically three types of dummy or feint.

1   *With the stick* — it is possible to indicate by using the stick that you are going to play the ball one way and then play it in an entirely different way.
- Beating an opponent by going right or left, e.g., the player plays over the ball with the stick slightly beyond the ball as though to move or pass to his left and suddenly reverses the ball and moves to his right (see photographs 6(a)-6(c) on page 76).
- When tackling, e.g., a tackler makes a dummy poke or lunge tackle but then retreats and waits for the player with the ball to make a move which has been forced onto him by the impending tackle. The tackler then tackles when he chooses the correct moment.
- When trapping — a right side player can prepare to trap the ball outside his left foot but allow it to run in front of his body and trap it by his right foot. Thus the opponent suddenly finds himself at an immediate disadvantage as the ball is now on his reverse side.
- When pushing, e.g., a player shapes to push in one direction, "showing" the ball to his or her opponent on the end of the stick, then quickly changes the direction of the push by changing the angle of his or her stick.

2   *With the ball* — by simply moving the ball to right or left and suddenly moving it in the opposite direction the ball can be used in a feint. Since defenders should be concentrating their attention solely on the ball this can be the most effective method of feinting. Similarly a player running with the ball can slow down (or stop) and then quickly continue. An opponent who is chasing will also slow down (or stop) and lose ground starting again.

3   *With the body* — the chapter on pushing demonstrated how a player could indicate the direction of a push by body positioning and then push elsewhere. (See photographs 4(a)-4(c) in chapter 3.) Similarly with hitting, trapping or tackling one may assume a particular posture without having any intention of following the course of action indicated by that posture. Also a body swerve while running in a particular direction is really a body feint or dummy which is used to deceive one's opponents.

There are of course many more examples of feinting which can be applied to most situations in a hockey match. Watching top class players in action one can easily appreciate the vast number of situations when feints or dummies can be used. However, it would also demonstrate that the best players only use feints when they are most necessary and can be most effective. Used sparingly they can be very devastating and a source of great confusion to any opponent.

A swerve (or body swerve) is a movement in which the body's weight is swayed (or indeed moved) to one side indicating that you are to change direction to that side. Suddenly you push off from that side and go in the opposite direction. It is really a feint using your body.

It should be noted that in order to go in one direction (e.g. to the right) around a player, the body's weight should first be shifted onto the opposite (e.g. left) leg in order to maintain power and balance when pushing off that leg.

Players should practise running and swerving around obstacles to perfect their footwork before attempting to do so with the ball. Photographs 6(a) and (b) in chapter 4 indicate how a player pushes off his left foot to go right and vice versa.

Feinting, swerving, etc. have been mentioned in this chapter because they have particular relevance to beating an opponent in man to man situations. However, all players should be aware that feints will be used against them. The following piece of advice is useful in dealing with such situations.

"When the ball is in close proximity your total concentration should be on the ball and nothing else. Allow your reflexes to take care of any movements you have to make but *don't anticipate* what your opponent *may* do. Remain balanced to move either way or retreat or lunge. When the ball is at a distance (e.g. greater than 15 metres) then allow *anticipation* to work for your advantage."

When do you beat an opponent?
One of the most difficult aspects of taking on an opponent is: "When should I do it?" The following are some situations in which it is appropriate to try to beat your immediate opponent:

1   When a forward breaks loose with one defender between that forward and the goal and with no team mate who he or she feels will be in a better position if passed the ball. A forward in such a situation should endeavour to beat that opponent and shoot with all haste.

2   During any game sometimes attempting to beat your opponent is a standard risk that all forwards should take when the opportunity presents itself. Success can create a numerical advantage or scoring opportunity for your team.

3   Defenders sometimes find themselves in a situation where they cannot find a pass to a forward and in order to retain possession must beat an onrushing opponent. It should be noted that they should only do so when everything is in their favour. Often it may be safer to clear over the side-line and surrender a push-in.

The simplest way
One should always use the simplest and least complicated way possible to eliminate an opponent. Usually that is by passing; sometimes it entails

pushing the ball past and following it up quickly. On other occasions you may choose to go to your opponent's right or left.

The simplest way besides passing entails merely pushing the ball (at controlled speed) past (or through) an opponent's legs and quickly running *around* your opponent to retrieve the ball. While this may sound simple, great skill is required and the following points bear mentioning:

1 Don't push the ball too far or fast — you will not get it before a covering defender or the ball goes out of play.

2 Run *around*, don't run into your opponent — your aim should be to avoid her or him and get the ball.

3 If you can outmanoeuvre your opponent first, you will be more efficient at beating that opponent. By shaping or feinting to go right or left you can usually then slip the ball between their legs or on their reverse while they are expecting something else.

Photographic sequence 2(a)-2(e) shows this skill being performed at practice by Richard Charlesworth, opposed by Australian fullback Craig Davies.

(a) Charlesworth looks to be going to Davies' right.

(b) and (c) Suddenly he opens the face of his stick and pushes the ball just past Davies' left foot.

(d) and (e) He avoids Davies and reaches the ball.

2a

2b

2c

2d

2e

3

Photograph 3 is a further demonstration of this skill by two schoolboy players. This time the ball has been played through the tackler's legs and the player in light shorts has gone around his opponent's left side.

A further extension of this skill is the ability of a player who is about to be challenged (from the side), to push the ball ahead of himself into a space and accelerate quickly onto it. Thus his opponent is cut out as he comes in to tackle.

Similarly the ball can be played through a gap between two opponents and then by quick acceleration through the gap it can be regained and controlled.

Photograph 4 provides an excellent example of this. Taken during the semi-final of the 1976 Olympics in Montreal, Australia's right inner, Richard Charlesworth, is just inside the scoring circle and confronted by Pakistan's fullbacks, Munewaraz Zaman (left), and Mansoor-ul-Hassan (right). He seizes the opportunity to push the ball between them as he is about to push off through the gap using his left leg. Charlesworth retrieved the ball before it crossed the backline and was able to cross pass to a team mate who scored.

4

5

Beating an opponent by going right

The great advantage of going right rather than left is that your opponent is usually put in a situation where he must make a reverse stick tackle.

Photograph 5 depicts Richard Charlesworth going on the right of Canada's left fullback Alan Hobkirk. Hobkirk has turned to make a tackle with his reverse yet Charlesworth seems to be well past with the ball under control.

6a

6b

6c

Now, using a photographic sequence, we can break up such a manoeuvre into its component parts. Australia's right inner, Marian Alymore, shows how an opponent can be outmanoeuvred and eliminated by going right.

In photographs 6(a)-(c),

(a) Marian has the ball under control and looks to be moving to her left as Diane Walsh moves in to tackle.

(b) Suddenly Marian reverses the ball and changes direction while maintaining good balance.

(c) By the time Diane has made her adjustment it is too late. Marian is going past and Diane is left to make a difficult reverse stick tackle. By feinting over the ball and swerving as though going left Marian was able to "wrong foot" or outmanoeuvre Diane and give herself room on her right into which she could move. Then with change of speed (acceleration) and change of direction, good timing and sound dribbling skills she completes the elimination.

7

Finally, photograph 7 shows Dutch player Cees-Ja Dieperveen as he reverses the ball and changes direction rapidly to avoid Abdul Rashid (4) of Pakistan, who is preparing to tackle. Rashid, by being front-on, is not in a good position to tackle or retreat and looks to be getting himself into a position where he will make a difficult reverse stick tackle.

Beating an opponent by going left

The same principles apply as for going right, except that the tackler being on the flat stick side is usually able to tackle more easily. Again an initial deception or feint can hand the advantage to the player with the ball by putting the tackler out of position or off balance.

Even though it is very difficult, the player should endeavour to keep the ball on the flat stick side if it is at all possible. If he or she finds that the tackler is likely to succeed the ball can then be moved onto the reverse stick side to provide extra width away from the tackler's stick. If, however, the ball is initially put on the reverse then there is no scope for such adjustments to be made.

Photographs 8(a)-8(d) on page 78 demonstrate Richard Charlesworth being tackled by Craig Davies and going to his left.

(a) Charlesworth shows the ball as though to pass right or push through Davies' legs.

(b) Once Davies is committed, Charlesworth suddenly moves to his left with the ball and

(c) makes a special attempt to keep the ball on his flat stick still keeping Davies in his peripheral vision.

(d) Almost beyond Davies he has moved to cut him out by getting back into his initial line.

8a

8b

8c

8d

9a

9b

9c

9d

Photographic sequence 9(a)-(d) shows some similar action. However, this time Charlesworth after making his initial move finds Davies is too close and so moves the ball over to his reverse. Thus, in (c), he gives himself more room and in photograph (d) has almost achieved his aim of passing Davies by going left.

Again the essential elements are:

1   Initial deception (feint and/or swerve)

2   Rapid change of speed and direction

3   Timing of movements

4   Good balance

5   Knowing what's ahead (scanning)

6   Sound dribbling skills

All these elements play a part in the elimination of any opponent in a man to man situation. One other aspect which deserves mention is *variation*. Any opponent will soon work out what is going on if the same methods are employed every time. Only by varying your play can you keep an opponent guessing. If he or she is worried as to whether you will pass, push past, go right or left, he or she will never approach you with any certainty.

Practice exercises

Those exercises relevant to dribbling are of great value and should be drilled thoroughly.

1   *Without the ball,* practise using correct footwork to change direction and speed by avoiding obstacles slalom style. You may wish to use moving obstacles, i.e. a line of players walking slowly towards the runner spaced at eight metre intervals. Once the previous runner reaches the other end and joins the line of walking players, the end player peels off and turns to run slalom style through the walkers. Thus players from one end continually run through the walkers and join on at the other end.

2   *With the ball,* practise avoiding obstacles slalom style. Then try going on the right of the line of obstacles which are staggered so each is two metres to the right of the last. Come in the other direction, going left each time.

3   Make a number of "gates" approximately 50 centimetres wide using stakes or witches' hats. These should be staggered and approximately 10 metres apart. Each player should practise approaching the gates and pushing the ball through the gate and retrieving it on the other side. Be sure you run around and not through the gate.

    Then make up a drill whereby each player receives the ball, breaks right or left, goes through a gate, and on controlling the ball on the other side shoots at goal. This closely simulates a situation that all forwards find themselves in at some time.

4   *Tackling:* Incorporate tackling practice with dribbling and beating an opponent. Firstly a group of five or six with one tackler as they practise beating him one by one. The tackler can initially be passive (merely a wide obstacle!) and then become a serious tackler. Players should experiment but remember the simplest way is usually the best.

5   *Small games:*
    - Three players — three goals in a triangle. Each player can attack his or her opponent's goal while defending his or her own. You must take risks to score and this is good practice at beating an opponent.
    - In a confined space two onto two. To score you must eliminate an opponent by combined passing and/or beating an opponent by feinting or dummying on your team mate. Again you must take risks and be positive.

9   Position play

This has undoubtedly been the most difficult chapter to write because there is so much that could be written about every position on the field. Also, over recent years many variations on the traditional pyramid system have been instituted in different countries by various teams.

For the purposes of this book we have adopted the orthodox (or pyramid) system because it is the major formation used in this country. However, it is important to realise that with only a few relatively minor changes that formation, as we play it in Australia, can be almost indistinguishable from many of those used in Europe. Many of the basic concepts of "cover defence", "marking", "running into space", "overlapping" etc., apply to hockey as a whole rather than any particular team formation or system. Also, it should be realised that no team formation will be successful without a team of players who have mastery of the basic skills of the game. It is the quality of the individuals that will decide the fate of the system used.

Basically the pyramid system provides for five attackers or forwards and six defenders. It is false, however, to consider any player solely an attacker or defender. Indeed all players should immediately become defenders once the opposition gain possession and until possession is regained. Likewise, many a goalkeeper's clearance has produced a goal at the opposite end of the field. All players are attackers when their team has possession!

The roles of a player in any position are relatively clearly defined but it is essential to allow for every player's versatility and flexibility. There is no reason why a defender cannot fulfil a forward's role at some stage in a game and vice versa. Similarly, interchange of positions can occur without disruption to the system or style of play and players should be encouraged to experiment.

We have made use of "player tracking" to give young readers some indication of *where* they should be positioned on the field during a match. These diagrams are simply a representation of all the movements of certain top players during a particular time span of a game. Often young players are told to play in particular "lanes" on the field. We believe this is unrealistic for all but the very young. Our tracking diagrams simply give an indication of *where* you should go without the rigid confinement that "lanes" often impose. Some of the diagrams also indicate what sort of passes a player gave and therefore provide some information of *how* to play a particular position. Young players will note that there are occasions when a right side player will be found on the left and vice versa.

For the most part we have tried to concentrate on *how* to play a position rather than *where* you should be. Each position has its characteristics, however, and it is impossible to expand on all of these, indeed it is not really within the stated intention of this book. We have endeavoured to present what we believe are the most vital aspects of each position and maybe also mention some facets to which a young player can aspire!

For beginning players

The young hockey player has much to remember and put into practice when he or she first plays in matches. It is essential that he or she should have a few basic ideas as to what is required. Too much information will only create confusion.

The following are guidelines for young hockey players:

1   *Use the full width and length of the field:* Too many games are spoilt by overcrowding. Following the ball all the time makes for crowded play and even if you get it there is often no room to move or do anything useful with it. By playing the ball to your wings whenever possible you create room or space on the field and of course encourage the winger to stay out wide as he or she has no need to come infield to get it.

2   *Know the three or four most important aspects of your position:* With time and experience you will quickly learn more about your position, but to start with concentrate on doing the few most important things well rather than trying to do everything.

3   *Try a number of positions:* Just as a twelve year old school child seldom knows what he wants to do for a career, it is absurd to expect the beginning hockey player to decide on a position for the rest of his playing days. He or she must first experience the possibilities which are available. Use your many practice and match situations to try different positions and always when watching top class players note how they fulfil their respective roles.

4   *All positions are important:* The belief that some positions are of much more importance than others stems from the fact that generally the ball is handled more by some positions than others (e.g. right inner and right wing). However we should realise that it is the quality of our play rather than the quantity that is of most importance. It has already been suggested that the goalkeeper is of tremendous importance to any team yet few players ever touch the ball less than a goalkeeper. Remember the *quality* of your play is more important than the *quantity*.

5   *Learn from your mistakes:* After playing a match make a critical assessment of your performance as to whether or not you achieved your aims. Did I play the position as I intended? If not, why not? Always discuss difficult situations which may have arisen. The best way to learn about any position is to experience the difficulties involved in playing it. Something will always occur which you had not anticipated and only by having to deal with such occurrences and discussing them with the coach will you learn thoroughly.

The positions
In the orthodox system the 11 players are deployed:
Five forwards — two wingers, left and right
                — two inside forwards, left and right
                — one centre forward
Three halfbacks — two wing halves, left and right
                — one centre half
Two fullbacks — left and right
One goalkeeper (discussed in detail in chapter 10)

The forwards
The basic aim of the forwards collectively and as individuals is to *"create*

1

scoring opportunities and from these score goals". There are no restrictions, they can score as many goals as possible in each game! That is their aim.

What is essential is that the five forwards must *work together* in order to achieve this aim. Only by combined play, co-operation and understanding can their individual talents be fully realised. It is well known that one or two outstanding players can be blotted out by effective marking. However, a confident forward line using all its players, both sides of the field and well supported by its defence can overwhelm the tightest of defences.

Photograph 1: *Forwards must work together* — Pakistan's left wing, Samiullah, has broken away from his New Zealand opponent on the halfway line and is heading towards the goal. Notice that three other Pakistan forwards, Hanif (left inner), Mansoor Junior (right inner) and Kalimullah (right wing) are all running to get into attack with Samiullah while centre forward Hasan Sardar is ahead of the other four and out of the picture. By the time Pakistan reach the goal scoring circle there will be five forwards deployed to make use of any chances which are created.

Some of the most essential aspects of playing in the forward line are:

1   *Passing and receiving (trapping) the ball while on the move:* A forward who is invariably being watched by a defender must be able to take possession of the ball while on the move so as to allow more time to set up a pass. Similarly, the player must be able to scan the situation ahead and once an opening is seen, quickly send a pass away with accuracy and without breaking stride. There will also be many occasions when once having received the ball the forward will immediately pass to a

team mate and continue running into another position to receive a return pass.

2 *Speed of movement and thought:* This does not only apply to ability to run fast, which naturally can be of benefit to any hockey player. More importantly a forward must be able to sum up the situation and with speedy movement or passing be able to exploit it. Any defence can be hard to crack if it is given time to settle and prepare for the onslaught. Finally, there are many occasions when a forward can use anticipation to give advantage. Many times a goal is scored because a forward anticipated a defence error and capitalised on it.

3 *Goal shooting and rebounding:* This is an area too often neglected in these days of set play scoring. Young players should take every opportunity to shoot at goal rather than win a corner. Many types of shot are necessary in the repertoire of any forward. A hard hit, a controlled push, a flick high into the net all yield goals in different situations and all warrant practising. Young players should be discouraged from shooting when at an acute angle unless they aim to hit the goalkeeper knowing a team mate is waiting at the pads for a rebound.

Rebounding refers to a player's ability to pick up shots that are saved (usually by the goalkeeper) and push them back into the goal. Every forward will be confronted with rebounds at different times and without anticipating and being prepared for them many valuable scoring chances can be wasted. Practice with a tennis ball against a brick wall is useful to sharpen skills in this area.

4 *Dribbling skills:* These are no less important than the first three points and all forwards should become confident in their dribbling skills and ability to beat an opponent, or change direction and speed. During any game the forwards should test out the defence and vary their play by occasionally taking on an opponent in a man to man situation. Success often means a goal!

5 *Sometimes defenders:* Finally it should be mentioned that all forwards also have a defensive role to play. When the other team has possession they must become defenders and harass, chase and tackle until possession is regained. Then having gained possession they should be careful never to lose the ball by loose or slack play and so cause more pressure to be brought on their own defenders.

Photograph 2: *Tackling back* — Although New Zealand forward Geoff Archibald has been dispossessed he has turned and is about to "tackle back" on West Australian fullback Craig Davies. By putting Davies under pressure Archibald may well force him to give a hurried and inaccurate pass. Even if he is unable to get the ball himself, Archibald has made it easier for his team mate to intercept.

We will now look more closely at some of the particular facets of playing in a particular position in the forward line:

The wings

The wingers generally occupy the space closest to the sideline on their respective sides — right or left. Their use as often as possible allows for the opposition defence to be stretched to cover the full width of the field making

2

it more easily outmanoeuvred or split open. Attempting to charge straight down the middle of the field is invariably difficult but when the ball is quickly transferred out to a winger he or she often finds room in front. Given room, he or she should always make ground towards the goal as quickly as possible. If the immediate opponent (the wing half) has been eliminated by a pass or by the winger's own skill he or she should head towards the goal circle by cutting infield in an arc and so cut out the wing half who is trying to get back into defence. Should the wing who is cutting in be confronted by another defender he or she then still has the option of going wide again if wished. Any such breakaway should be completed with a firm accurate pass (or "centre") to another forward with a shot at goal.

By involving its wingers in passing movements and allowing them scope to be part of most attacks, a team is able to keep the opposition guessing as to the position and method of each attack.

Diagram A on page 86 is a player tracking diagram of Pakistan's famous left wing Samiullah, taken in a game against Holland in 1980. The dotted lines represent Samiullah's centres. Note:

1   He seldom if ever comes back inside his own 25 metre line in defence.

2   He seldom gets into the left-hand corner of the field in attack as there is little that can be done from that corner. On all his runs with the ball he tends to "cut in" an arc rather than running parallel to the sideline and allowing opponents to tackle back.

3   Sometimes the ball is centred well before the circle. Sometimes it is passed immediately it is received. Remember variety is important in all you do!

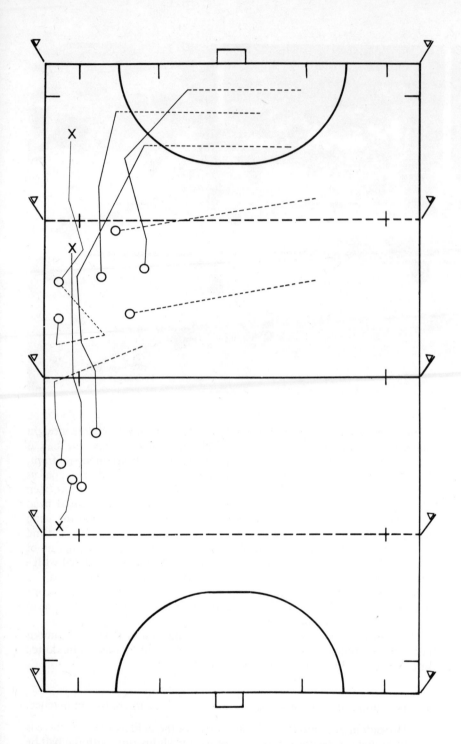

Diagram A
PAKISTAN v. HOLLAND
(1st half)
Pakistan Left Wing Samiullah

X = *Tackled and dispossessed*
O = *Received the ball*
— = *Running with the ball*
--- = *Pass or centred ball*

While this is only a diagrammatic representation it does give some idea of *where* a winger is deployed and the sort of places he runs and passes.

What makes a good winger?
The following are some of the most important atttributes of any winger:

1   *Speed:* Any break made at speed in a passing sequence or alone can be a potential goal. Again, quick thinking and quick running are of equal importance. You must be able to run fast and keep the ball under control. Any prospective winger should practise running fast with the ball under control.

2   *Trapping:* By trapping the ball correctly many a winger is able to put the defender at a disadvantage. Practise trapping on the move with a defender in front of you — it is difficult, but essential for any wing.

   Photographs 3(a)-3(d): Australian winger, Terry Walsh, demonstrates one method whereby the right wing can gain advantage over his left half by allowing the ball to run across his body as he traps it.

   (a)   Walsh feints as though he will take the ball but then
   (b)   allows it to run *across* in front of him till finally stick and ball make contact.

3a

3b

3c

3d

(c) He is now on the left half's reverse stick side and quickly moves down the line to take advantage of the situation.

(d) The same technique can of course be employed on the left half's side where a left side player can similarly "wrong foot" his opponent. It is of course generally less successful as the ball is then on his opponent's flat stick side.

3 *Centring:* To centre the ball effectively from either wing is the traditional view of a winger's role. It is a skill which comes with practice and concentration. These things are important.

- *A hard hit* — although not always used, powerful centres are very often required.
- *Look before you centre* — you should know where your team mates should be but a look always helps you find them and avoids defenders.
- *Vary your centres* — you have already seen how Samiullah varied his centring.
- *Wait for the correct time* — if you want to centre but the situation isn't right then don't be afraid to wait or go on further yourself. Passes to nobody are of no use to your team.

4 *Anticipation:* When the play is on the opposite side of the field a good winger will occasionally seize the opportunity to cut infield and lead or pick up a pass. This applies particularly around the circle where many a winger has scored from a centre from the opposite side.

5   *Goal scoring ability:* Know when to shoot and when to pass and always look out for rebounds or deflections.

6   *Defence:* Once possession is lost the wingers should start moving back towards their own goal. If the ball is in their immediate vicinity they should chase hard and back tackle but if it is not they should make sure their opposing wing half isn't able to make a contribution to his team's attack.

Finally, it is worth mentioning that there are of course differences between playing left and right wing. These are mainly concerned with how we trap the ball and are covered in the chapter on trapping. Also, the ball should be carried differently on the left side when dribbling.

4

Photograph 4 shows India's left wing Syed Ali in the classical pose of a left wing, preparing to centre the ball. The left wing should endeavour to keep the ball on the flat stick side so as to be able to survey the whole field before passing. Notice how Syed Ali has his body well outside the ball as he scans across the field and prepares to pass.

The inside forwards

Of all the forwards the insides have a greater role in the midfield. They are often considered merely as receivers and passers of the ball but while this is of course an essential part of their game, a good inside will do much more.

While the problem for the winger is "where will the ball come from?", for the inside it is "where shall I pass it?".

The inside often has more than one pass available and must decide which is best or whether he or she should carry the ball, engage or involve a defender and then pass or attempt to beat an opponent. Generally the passes will be about evenly distributed between the wing, the centre forward and the opposite inner with some also going to a halfback running on. It should be noted of course that once a pass is given that player will often run on to complete a triangular movement. These pieces of play with wing or centre forward or even centre half or wing half can open large gaps in any defence.

The insides' role in attack, midfield and defence calls for a high work rate and diagram B gives an illustration of this. It shows 15 minutes of play by Australia's right inner, Richard Charlesworth, in the final of the Esanda World Tournament in Perth, 1979. Note:

1 Generally Charlesworth occupied the area right of centre with occasional movements out towards the wing and infield.

2 Once he was as far in defence as his own defensive circle, yet four times he crossed the opposition circle in that time (once to take a push out for a penalty corner). He spent more time in the attacking half than his team's defensive half.

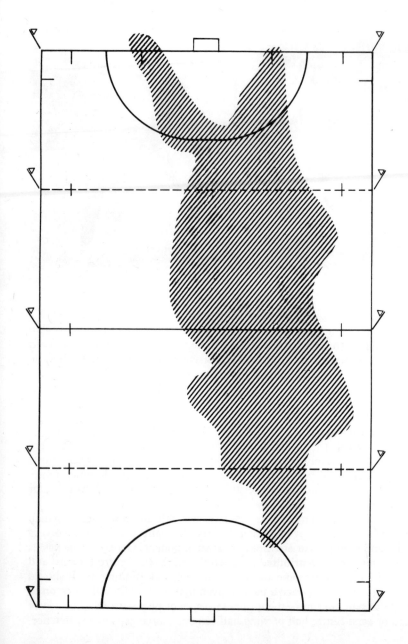

Diagram B
AUSTRALIA v. Pakistan
(15-20 minutes)

Australian Inside Right, R. Charlesworth

What makes a good inside forward?

The following are the important aspects of inside forward play:

1   *Passing ability:* To make the right pass at the right time is probably the most important ability for an inside forward to possess. The inside forward should have a strategy in mind and work on keeping the defence guessing as to what will happen next. Passing movements involving those around him or her (wing, centre forward, halves) can be mixed with through and cross passes.

2   *Receiving and breaking away:* As the inside is often surrounded by players he or she must develop the ability to receive the ball from different angles and break clear with sudden bursts of speed or change of direction.

3   *Work rate:* To be in the defensive circle one minute and the attacking circle the next requires fitness and a willingness to work for the team. In any match, periods for rest will occur. These should be utilised to the full.

4   *Dribbling skills:* When the opportunity presents itself, an inside forward must be able to "take on" his fullback. This is often possible after a quick transference of play and if successful the inside will often be able to enter the circle and shoot.

5

Photograph 5 depicts Richard Charlesworth "going around" left fullback Lindsay Mullings in an A grade grand final. Mullings makes a desperate dive to halt Charlesworth because he knows that now Charlesworth has a clear passage to goal.

At some time during a game any inside forward should "test out" the opposing fullback by taking him on. If successful, then he or she may get a chance to score. Even if the test fails, the fullback will have another possibility to contend with next time that forward has the ball.

5   *Goal shooting:* Both insides will be presented with chances to score. They should be adept at shooting hard from the top of the circle as well as flicking and pushing from close range. Generally the left inside seems to get more chances as most sides attack more down the right and cross the ball to the left in the circle. Also, to trap and shoot is slightly easier from the left side.

6   *Defence:* Whenever possible an inside should cover the opposing inside — sometimes by close marking, at other times by covering the line between the ball and opponent. However, no inside should be expected to run great distances and expend energy needlessly to do this task. Insides should practise tackling, intercepting, marking and tackling back as they will be required to perform all these in fulfilling this defensive role.

As with the wing positions there are many differences in trapping, dribbling and passing between the right and the left side of the field. These are generally covered in other chapters and no space will be devoted to them here except to say that on the left side the reverse flick and reverse stick play are used more and should be practised.

The centre forward

The centre forward is the traditional leader of the forward line. While many believe the inners now fulfil this role, the centre forward can by leading and calling largely direct the pattern of play in any forward line.

The centre forward must be a goal scorer. As the player who is positioned directly in front of the goal — for that is where the centre forward should usually take up position in the circle — his or her scoring skills should be carefully honed to make the most of the chances made available.

What makes a good centre forward?

1   *Ability to receive and pass from and to both sides:* As the centre forward has insides and wingers on both sides and defenders behind he or she must be adept at receiving balls from all directions and passing it in all directions. He or she must be proficient, for example, at receiving the ball from the left and quickly reversing it to his or her right inner with a reverse stick pass and vice versa. The centre forward must be able to trap on reverse and flat stick sides while on the move. This is particularly relevant when getting involved in short passing sequences with inside forwards, as he or she should always be endeavouring to do.

2   *Scoring of goals:* As the person best positioned to score on most occasions the centre half must have a strong shot at goal. He or she must also be skilful at trapping the ball in the circle and quickly getting in a push or flick shot. On many occasions the role involves picking up rebounds from other players' shots and he or she must anticipate and forever be the opportunist.

3   *Leading and changing direction:* The centre forward should not be afraid to lead out of the middle to create a space for himself or herself. However when leading forward he or she must take care not to run offside. Should she or he lead one way and not receive the ball, the centre forward can sometimes quickly change direction and lead back to from where he or she came. Similarly, when marked sudden movement in one direction followed by a change of direction will enable him or her to lose the marker.

4   *Dribbling skills:* The centre forward will often find situations where there is one defender to beat for a shot at goal. He or she should try to pass to an inside if one is available but on many occasions the centre forward must take on the defender or goalkeeper and attempt to score.

5   *Defensiveness:* The centre forward like all other forwards should harass and tackle back when possession is lost. His or her particular responsibility will often be the centre half of the opposition, who must not be allowed to control the game.

The halfbacks

The halfbacks are essentially *defenders* who must also play a part in many attacking moves by providing the link between attack and defence. Their first responsibility is to defend and then they should attack with discretion and only when such movement is most appropriate. For this reason they must be able to "read the play" and assess the tide of the game correctly (with five minutes to go and a one goal lead they should not be pressing for another goal at the risk of weakening their own defence).

What makes a good halfback?

1   *Interception and trapping:* Whereas a mistrap by a forward is seldom dangerous, such a mistake in the defence can cost a goal. The halfbacks must be sound, safe trappers of the ball and should if possible make sure they get behind the ball so their eye is over it as they trap. By reading the play and sound trapping they can make many interceptions and thus put their team back into attack.

2   *Tackling:* Any half will be required to make a number of tackles during a game. The technique for right and left will be different but the principles of being side-on, balanced, alert and ready to retreat are all valid.

3   *Passing:* Only very occasionally should a halfback find it necessary to take on an opponent. Almost every time possession is gained he or she should immediately look to distribute to a forward. The pass should usually be a *quick, obvious* one and most times it will be a *push* flat along the ground to make an easy trap for the forward. There will of course be situations where a long pass must be hit (e.g. to an inside on the other side of the field) or where a through pass can be given for a forward to run on to.

4   *Willingness to attack:* When appropriate a halfback should play a part in attacking moves by running alongside or even occasionally ahead (overlapping) into spaces so as to make an *extra forward*. If done correctly this can occur without in any way lessening his or her defensive effectiveness.

5   *Hard working:* Much of a halfback's job is to make position without actually getting the ball. Often he or she must run to cover a team mate just in case something happens or a halfback may mark his or her opponent in order to discourage a pass being given. Sometimes he or she will lend him or herself to an attack and not be used. All this running and movement necessitate that halfbacks be very fit and willing to work hard for the team.

6

Photograph 6: *Halfbacks running to make themselves available* — Final Australian championships, 1977 — result, WA(3) v NSW (0). Left fullback Craig Davies has the ball and is "looking" up field for a pass — notice Craig is preparing to push the ball rather than hit. More interesting are the movements of Craig Boyce (4) left half and David Bell (3) centre half. Both are moving into position in case Craig should find it necessary to use them. Craig Boyce, by running away and towards the sideline, will provide a safe pass for Davies should none be available further up field.

The centre half

The centre half essentially confines his or her area of influence to the middle of the field from circle to circle. He or she will only very rarely be found on the wing and then only in extreme circumstances or when he or she has interchanged with a wing half for the same reason.

This player is, as already stated, a defender first and as such he or she should always endeavour to keep the play in front — seldom will a good centre half be found running back into the play. Usually the play has to come to him or her. When the play goes to either wing the centre half simply turns to face it confident in the knowledge that generally the ball comes back into the middle for an effective shot at goal. When that occurs he or she will get the chance to tackle or intercept. Strong discipline is required in order not to get "drawn" out of the middle.

Diagram C
AUSTRALIA v. PAKISTAN
(20 minutes)

Pakistan Centre Half, Aktar Rasool

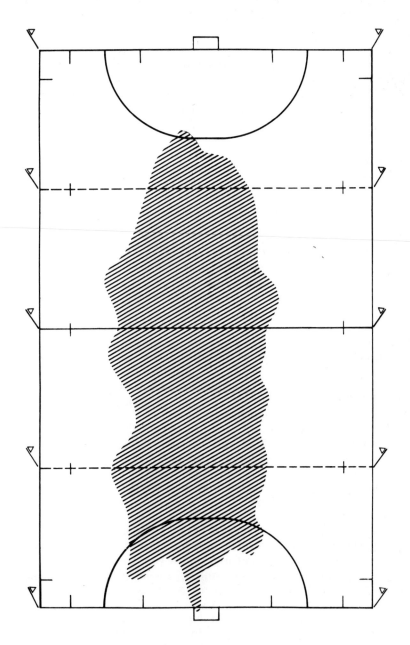

Diagram C illustrates the area of the field patrolled by Pakistan's centre half, Aktar Rasool, during a match. Note:

1   Seldom does Aktar find it necessary to run wide from the centre of the field, which he patrols with great discipline.

2   Aktar travels from his defensive circle to the attacking circle during the game but generally spends more time in the defensive half of the field.

3   He is also called upon to handstop for penalty corners in attack and to defend such corners on the goal-line for his team.

By maintaining the position in the centre, the centre half enables the rest of the defence to swing around him or her as the pivot. Generally they are able to use the centre half as a marker and only when he or she is in position will the fullbacks commit themselves fully to a tackle on their inners.

Once the centre half comes into possession, he or she should immediately look to distribute, usually to an inner, but also on occasions to wings with a hard accurate hit or to either halfback should a forward not be available. Most of his or her passes will be pushes and the centre half must learn to conceal the intended direction of each pass so as to give the forwards more time to control the ball.

During an attack the centre half can often be used to relay the ball from one side of the field to another. More importantly he or she should "read the play" so as to immediately get into the open when his or her side wins possession of the ball. The centre half can thus be the springboard of many attacks.

The wing halves

The most important function of a wing half is to stop opposing wingers from playing an effective part in the game. They should work in unison and develop an understanding with their respective fullbacks, so if one of them is beaten the other provides cover allowing the beaten player time to recover and rejoin the defence.

Generally *when the ball is in close proximity* the wing half should be close to his or her winger in a position where ball and wing can be seen and be a couple of metres closer to his or her own goal than the wing. He or she should endeavour to intercept (if possible) any pass to the wing or at least interfere with the control and concentration of the wing by being close by and tackling as the wing attempts to trap the ball.

When the play is at a distance the wing half can afford to be further from the wing because even if a long pass is given he or she will have more time to move to that wing or intercept. Indeed, when the ball is on the other side he or she can afford to be infield merely covering the line of a pass to his or her winger. Many wing halves can be found at about the position of the inside forward and by their presence they distract any pass to that player from the other side of the ground.

Note: Such play is only recommended once you become experienced in recognising when you can be infield or away from your wing and when you should be close to him or her. Similarly, should your wing lead across the field the wing half must follow until you feel the wing has run into the centre half's territory or until an interchange is seen occurring and another player is in the winger's position.

Trapping and tackling are of paramount importance to any wing half. As a general rule a wing half should never allow his or her wing to get past him or her on the outside (i.e. between wing half and the side line). It is usually better to force your wing to run infield thus crowding the attack and limiting the range of opportunities. This is particularly correct on the left side where a left half will often position him or herself with heels on the sideline and thereby force his or her right wing infield and so enable him or herself to tackle on the flat stick side. He or she should avoid having to make reverse stick tackles at any time. The right half's role is slightly different and there will be occasions when he or she will allow his or her left wing to run on the outside and thereby play him or herself into the attacking left corner from which it is very difficult to centre the ball or pass.

Once in possession, the wing halves should immediately be looking to pass to an awaiting forward; most often their inside forward, wing or the centre

Diagram D
AUSTRALIA v. INDIA
(20 minutes)

Indian Left Half, Bhaskaran

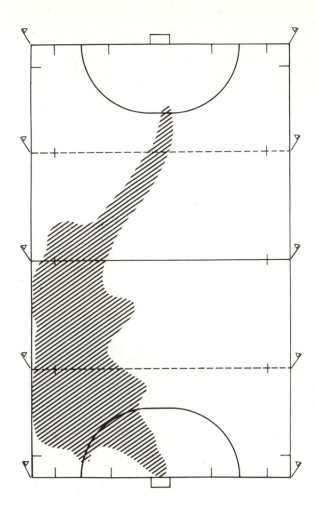

forward or a hard cross pass to the opposite inner. There will also be occasions when the centre half should be passed the ball as he or she is often in a better position to distribute to both sides of the field.

Of course once a pass has been given that is not the end of the wing half's role. If it is clear that the forward will win possession then the wing half should link up with his or her forwards in order to make an extra attacker. By becoming involved in passing movements the wing half can help eliminate the opposition defenders. A classical example is the right half and right inner using a triangular pass to beat the left fullback. Immediately any attack looks like breaking down or an interception is made the wing half should resume his or her defensive role as quickly as possible. It is important that the wing half be able to "read" or anticipate such situations as or before they occur. Traditionally the right half has been more attacking than the left half but the left half will also find moments when he or she can be a very effective support attacker.

Diagram D is a tracking diagram of Indian left half Bhaskaran during their game against Australia. Note:

1 Bhaskaran basically occupies the left-hand side of the ground in his own defensive half. Yet he is involved in occasional sorties into the opposite half.

2   He goes to the top of the circle in attack three times to handstop penalty corners and on three occasions he is positioned in his own goal where his job is to defend on the post for his team. (Any player in any position can of course fulfil these roles.)

3   Bhaskaran often moves infield into the circle to cover when the ball has moved down the other side of the field. Thus his movements are often arc-like as are those of most wings around the circle.

The fullbacks

The right and left fullback positions are more or less a mirror image of one another in their movements. Yet again there are differences in the type of trapping, tackling and passing most often required on each side. Both must understand what the other is doing and together they must work as a unit covering for one another and for their halfbacks if necessary.

Their immediate opponents are the inside forwards of the opposition. They should tackle the inside on their side, whenever he or she has possession and is moving towards the scoring circle. The wing halves and centre half have the function of looking after the wingers and centre forward. This tackling must only be undertaken when the halfbacks and other fullback are in position with their opponents under surveillance or marked. A fullback who rushes to tackle his inner without his fellow defenders in position will leave gaps through which the opposition can penetrate. An alert inner will recognise and exploit these gaps. Often the fullback's function will be merely to delay his or her inner. Sometimes by moving to tackle the inner he or she will force that player to pass. In doing that the fullback has served the first part of his or her function but once the inner passes the ball off, the fullback must be aware that the ball may go back to that inner. The job of defending is not over until the fullback's team has possession. Then there may be some way in which the fullback can assist the attack.

What makes a good fullback?

1   *Tackling ability:* The good fullback will try to tackle when the forward least expects it. By meeting the inner as he or she is receiving the ball he or she can sometimes easily dispossess him. However this is often not possible and the forward has the ball under control when the tackle must be made. Attempt to baulk or poke and retreat so as to force the forward to make a move — then you can pounce.

Never rush at a forward in control.

Always tackle in a position that allows you to retreat with the forward should you fail.

2   *Trapping and intercepting:* Any trapping error by a fullback can mean a goal if exploited by alert forwards. Whenever time and the situation permit take care to make a "safe" trap by getting well in line with the ball. Of course sometimes you will have to reach and make a reflex trap away from your body.

One very important aspect of fullback play is intercepting passes from the opposition. Many times a forward will endeavour to pass just outside a fullback's reach to a team mate or on other occasions will endeavour to slip the ball through the fullback's legs for another player to run on to. Lightning reflexes can allow a fullback to intercept some of these passes. Also by positioning him or herself in such a manner as to

Diagram E
AUSTRALIA v. INDIA
(2nd half, 25 minutes)

Australian Right Fullback, Jim
Irvine

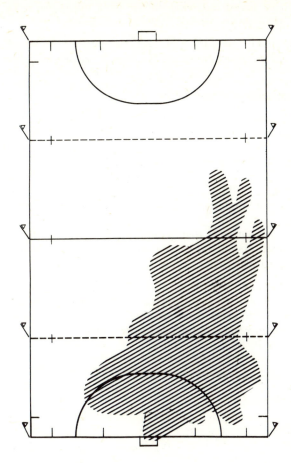

force the forward to pass where he or she wants the ball, a fullback can better intercept.

3 *Reading the play — covering in defence:* Generally when the play is in the forward area the fullback on that side is further up field than his or her other fullback who tends to move into the middle and behind the "up" fullback. Should the play change sides so the "up" fullback will fall away and the "back" fullback move "up" field.

Similarly, when the ball is on either side of the field, the other fullback must be prepared to come right across and clear any pass that is put behind the "up" fullback. It is necessary for the covering player to move with speed and assurance in such a situation. Any delay might mean an attacker reaching the ball first.

Of course should the wing half on the same side of the fullback be beaten again, that fullback must move out to tackle the winger (or whoever has broken through) while the wing half quickly recovers to fulfil the fullback's role. In the same way the wing half "covers" for a fullback who might be beaten by coming into tackle when necessary.

Diagram E shows a tracking diagram of Australian right fullback Jim Irvine in a match, Australia v India, 1979. Note:

• Jim is generally on the right side of the field but is often found across on the left when providing "cover" for his left fullback. Likewise he is *occasionally* to be found out wide on the wing making a tackle while the wing half "covers" inside, having been beaten.

- Seldom does Jim find it necessary to go over the centre-line in attack. However there are occasions when he is involved in play over the centre-line.

- Jim's task as a goal-line defender on penalty corners is also shown.

4 *Accurate and quick disposal:* Once in possession the ball should be quickly and without fuss delivered to the forwards with a push or firm hit.

Traditionally the fullbacks have been expected to hit the ball hard, as they have greater distances to cover and also can thereby get the ball furthest away from goal. While a powerful hit can be invaluable in many situations it is more important that the pass be taken quickly and that it be accurate.

Finally it should be mentioned that generally when clearing from a crowded circle the ball should be played wide so that even if it is intercepted the forward will have to shoot from an acute angle.

5 *Coolness:* The fullbacks should never get flustered and must endeavour to keep cool heads when playing in the deep defence. Any suggestion of panic can transmit itself to other team members and thereby threaten the stability of the defence and confidence of the whole team.

10 Goalkeeping

Some hockey followers may think it is a little unusual that a chapter of this book be devoted to one particular position — that of goalkeeper. However, this is the single most neglected area in hockey for young players. Too often the goalkeeper in a junior hockey team is the person who is the least mobile, least co-ordinated and least athletic member of that particular squad. As a consequence the position is looked upon as second-rate and lacking in real importance. Nothing could be further from the truth.

It is not the aim of this chapter to explain in great detail what a goalkeeper should do in every conceivable situation faced in a game of hockey. Rather, it is our intention to give the position the attention it deserves and give the young player a basic outline of the role and what it entails.

Goalkeeping is a vital skill

We ask the young player to consider why goalkeeping is so important.

Before the opposition scores a goal the goalkeeper must be passed.

The goalkeeper is the player who must attempt to save penalty corner hits and penalty strokes.

As the player with the whole field open to his or her gaze, the goalkeeper has a unique opportunity to direct the defence by constructive comments and instructions.

No other player is in a position to save a match as a goalkeeper must be. Good saves by the goalkeeper are frequently the difference between victory and defeat.

Too often the goalkeeper is the butt of team jokes, which sometimes can result in young players not choosing to play the position. However, the goalkeeper can be the continued focus of attention for courage, athletic ability and co-ordinated talents.

The goalkeeper's equipment

All goalkeepers should endeavour to obtain the correct playing gear because this gives them the confidence needed to attack potentially dangerous situations with surety. Study the well equipped goalkeeper in photograph 1 on page 102.

1 *Pads* — Note the thickness of these pads and their length, which affords protection to the entire leg.

2 *Gloves* — The size of the gloves shown is obviously not obligatory. Some goalkeepers prefer lighter less bulky types. However, the main point is that goalkeepers do protect their hands, giving them confidence in handstopping.

3 *Kickers* — Young players will notice that the kickers are large, well padded and well secured. If the goalkeeper is to perfect kicking skills then this is obviously of great necessity.

4   *Face mask* — This piece of equipment has not been in use for a long period, and indeed some goalkeepers still do not favour its usage. Face masks are perhaps a product of indoor hockey. However, they may provide a valuable aid in developing a young goalkeeper's confidence. Certainly a young keeper who doesn't wear a face mask should at least wear an approved mouth guard.

5   *Boots* — Hard toed boots provide extra protection when kicking the ball.

   In addition to what can be seen in the photograph, a goalkeeper often feels it necessary to wear extra support or padding to supplement the above four items. All goalkeepers of course should wear a "box" to protect the vital groin region just as any batsman at cricket wears such equipment. Under no circumstances should a goalkeeper be influenced into wearing too little protective gear by jibing team mates. Confidence is all-important to the young goalkeeper, and one way this can be gained is by using effective equipment.

Basic goalkeeping skills

Although there are obviously many skills components in an advanced goalkeeper's play, in this chapter we are merely aiming for a basis to

1

2

goalkeeping in order to encourage young players to try the position. We would choose the following three skills from the many a goalkeeper must eventually master. They are:

1   Trapping — by use of hand and foot.

2   Clearances — by foot or stick.

3   Positioning in the goal circle.

Trapping

A goalkeeper is expected to prevent the ball from entering the goal at all costs. Therefore the ability to stop or trap the ball at whatever height or speed it approaches is of paramount importance. Just as importantly, the goalkeeper should not allow the ball to rebound from the pads in such a way that opposing players can run in and gain possession. As we found in chapter 2, the ball must be actually trapped by the goalkeeper. The principles are basically the same as for a field trap. Watch left in photograph 2 how West Australian goalkeeper John Nettleton traps a low shot at goal.

John's back is bent as his head is over the ball watching it right onto his pads, which are tightly together.

John is well balanced on the balls of his feet so that he may quickly clear the ball.

John has his stick in his right hand — most goalkeepers prefer the right hand. This allows the goalkeeper to be well balanced and move freely. The young goalkeeper who holds his stick in both hands often moves sideways with a jumping movement and appears stilted as he is not able to use his arms freely in initiating his movements. Some goalkeepers prefer to hold the stick in the left hand, however this has obvious disadvantages when a quick one-handed clearance must be made.

Notice carefully how John's knees are bent, which cushions the ball and will prevent it from rolling out of his control.

Finally and very importantly, John like all good keepers has waited for the ball to come to him. A hurried jabbing action by the goalkeeper is fraught with danger as the resultant uncontrolled rebound may be snapped up by a goal hungry forward.

The same situation has occurred in photograph 3 where John was unable to get both pads to a shot and has saved with his left foot. He is still well balanced with his leg angled forward to trap the ball and he has again let the ball come to him rather than jabbing at it.

Clearances

The young goalkeeper should be conscious of one basic principle when making a clearance — to play the ball wide to the sidelines if at all possible. The reason for this is obvious, as it is much safer to clear the ball out of the way of advancing forwards. If opponents do block the clearance then they at least are forced to shoot from an acute angle.

However, the techniques of kicking with both feet are to be mastered before worrying unduly where the ball must go. Look carefully at

3

4

photographs 4 and 5 to see how John Nettleton concentrates on the following points:

In photograph 4 he is about to make contact and his body is perfectly balanced with his head directly over the ball.

John's right knee is forward of the ball to keep its trajectory low so he doesn't give away a penalty corner for dangerous play.

In photograph 5 we still see John's head over the ball, even though his leg is following through after having kicked the ball. Notice that John keeps his kicking leg coming straight through to prevent error.

5

As previously stated, goalkeepers should aim to clear the ball wide when kicking. As something to aim for watch in photograph 6 where Ian Taylor, the goalkeeper from Great Britain, makes a brilliant clearance during the 1979 World Hockey Tournament in Perth. Taylor is saving a short corner shot by swivelling on his left foot and kicking the ball over the sideline. This is a very advanced skill but demonstrates what can be achieved. Young players should note that Taylor, arguably the world's best goalkeeper, is demonstrating the same basic skills shown in our previous photographs.

In all instances so far discussed the goalkeeper can be noted to be using just pads and kickers. However, the stick is just as vital to a goalkeeper as a field player. Often when the ball is trapped by the pads the best method of clearance is by pushing or hitting the ball to the side of the field. Usually the goalkeeper is under pressure from opponents in this type of situation and must do things quickly but safely and have little or no margin for error. This

6

7

is graphically shown in photograph 7 by former West Australian goal-keeper Peter Shepherd.

Young goalkeepers should note the following points:

The ball has fallen in front of Peter's pads and he is under pressure from rival forwards Terry Walsh (right) and Gordon Clarke.

Still well balanced after making the initial trap, Peter is right over the ball and has bent more than double so that his right knee is on the ground giving him stability.

Notice how his hands are apart on his stick in excellent position to give power and precision to his push clearance (see chapter on pushing).

Peter's eyes still follow the path of the ball as he ensures it is safely away from the danger area.

Handstopping a shot at goal

The other most often used method of saving a shot at goal is by hand-stopping the raised ball. This is more often than not done by the left hand, keeping the stick firmly in the right hand, where it is of most potential benefit. The need will obviously arise to quickly change hands during some match situations. Photograph 8 shows John Nettleton executing this skill with his body behind the flight of the ball and eyes firmly fixed on its path to be followed after handstopping. John is well balanced to clear the ball once the handstop has been made. Photograph 9 shows the 1979 Indian goalkeeper saving at training with his right hand.

8

9

Positioning for goalkeepers

It is absolutely vital for a goalkeeper to be aware of the position he or she has adopted in relation to where the goals are. A large slice of training time should be directed towards this end (see exercises in this chapter). A goalkeeper, by astute positioning can narrow the angle available for shooting at goal by opponents. In photograph 10 below, note how the New Zealand goalkeeper in the 1979 World Hockey Tournament has moved close to his goal post when the play has obviously moved at a wide angle to his goals. He is concentrating on the play but is well balanced to make a compensating movement should the pattern of play be altered.

Most fields have the penalty spot marked seven yards (6.4 metres) from the backline and in the centre of the goals — this landmark can be used by the goalkeeper to quickly ascertain his position when he has had to move around the circle quickly and doesn't have time to turn and check his position. Also, by moving a few metres off the goal-line a goalkeeper can narrow the angle of an attacker about to shoot. With experience he will learn when it is most advantageous to do so.

The slide tackle

This is a skill which is present in the repertoire of every good goalkeeper. When the occasion presents itself the goalkeeper can very effectively dispossess or block a forward with this technique. It requires a high degree of timing and reading of the play.

As the young goalkeeper should firstly become proficient at the many other techniques involved in goalkeeping this is only mentioned for the sake of completeness. Remember it is better to err by staying in the goal (you still must be passed) rather than to leave a forward an open goal to shoot at because of your desire to rush out and *slide!* The slide can be spectacular and effective but its correct use can only be learnt by much competition, observation and practice.

10

What must a goalkeeper be?

Because of extra equipment he or she must be earlier to training and matches than team mates.

Goalkeepers must be thorough about the preparation and wearing of their equipment.

Goalkeepers must be mentally alert all through a match whether directly involved or not.

Goalkeepers must be constructive talkers at team meetings and during the match.

A confident goalkeeper is essential if a defence is to be confident as a unit.

A goalkeeper must not worry if a goal has gone through — it is the next shot which must be saved.

Training exercises for goalkeepers

Warm-up procedures

It is essential that goalkeepers follow a rigid routine of exercises which increase agility and flexibility. As with a field player, each muscle group should be stretched individually and attention should be paid to back flexibility (see chapter on correct preparation for a match). Particularly important for the goalkeeper are the groin and adductor muscles (inside of thigh). These are called upon in many "saving" situations. John can be seen stretching them in photograph 12. Photographs 11 and 12 on page 110 suggest some exercises for goalkeepers to try. There are obviously many more which can be done. However, "warm up thoroughly" before beginning other skills is the real message.

Skills exercises

1   Kicking practices where balls are pushed, hit, flicked at the goalkeeper who must trap with foot or hand only (not stick) and then quickly clear. Vary the pace of the shots at goal and the direction so that both feet and both hands are used.

2   The same exercise, however introduce two attackers who come in towards the goalkeeper and attempt to dispossess through rebounds. This places required pressure on the goalkeeper to trap the ball properly.

3   Place a right winger, centre forward and left winger in the scoring circle area in position they would normally assume in games. They shoot at quick intervals forcing the goalkeeper to quickly adjust position to counter the changed angles. This develops speed and an understanding of goal position.

4   Tackling of forwards who run into the circle and attempt to beat the goalkeeper is on the same principle as tackling as a basic skill. (See chapter 5. Goalkeepers should read this chapter carefully.)

5   Set play practice is vital. Defend penalty corners, corners and penalty strokes at almost every training session. The young goalkeeper should be encouraged *not* to anticipate in these situations — allow your reflexes to develop and take care of these set plays.

These are but a few of the many exercises goalkeepers can do. Like other players they must practise skills to succeed. A whole book could perhaps be devoted to the goalkeeper, but it is at least a beginning if young players really appreciate the value of an efficient goalkeeper. Goalkeepers should not be neglected and should themselves be proud of their importance to hockey.

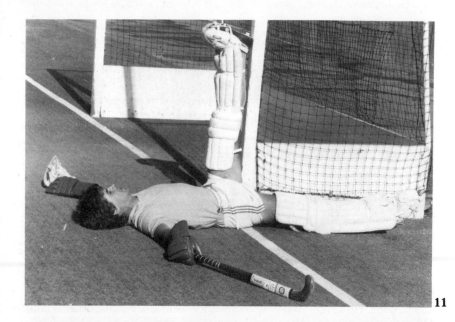

11

12

11 The basic rules of hockey

This chapter will not attempt to give a comprehensive explanation of the rules which govern the game of hockey. The aim is to give the young player a brief outline of some of the most common situations which occur in hockey which require the umpires to make a ruling. In no way are the comments to be taken as being a definite statement of what should or should not be the rules of the game as would be stated in a conventional rule book.

Respect the rules of hockey

It is most important that young players respect the rules of the game. Without this respect hockey will be the ultimate loser. If the control exerted by an umpire breaks down, so does the game and the players will therefore suffer. Remember that the umpire has a difficult job, and usually is giving up valuable personal time to perform what is almost always a thankless task. The best way to understand this difficulty is to umpire regularly yourselves. By volunteering to umpire as often as possible you can add to your understanding of the game and perform a useful service at the same time. Hockey needs a continual supply of keen and knowledgeable umpires. Play your part by playing, and helping out with umpiring when requested.

Commonly broken rules

1 Offside

A newcomer to the game often has difficulty understanding the offside rule. Quite simply, if a player does not have either the ball or two opposition players between him or her and the goal-line at the time the ball is moved by a team mate then that player is offside. Note photographs 1 and 2 which feature Brian Glencross, Richard Charlesworth, Craig Davies and goalkeeper John Nettleton. In photograph 1, Brian has passed the ball to team mate Richard. Craig, in the dark shirt and light shorts, waits to tackle Richard, backed by goalkeeper John. Richard is obviously not offside.

1

2

3

In photograph 2 Brian has again pushed the ball to Richard, but this time only goalkeeper John is between Richard and the goal-line. Therefore Richard is clearly offside.

2 Obstruction
A player may not place any part of his stick or body in such a position as to prevent an opponent from being able to play the ball. Not being able to shield the ball in such a manner is one of the major differences between hockey and soccer. Note the following two examples of body and stick obstruction. In photograph 3 see how Terry Walsh (black shorts) clearly obstructs Richard Charlesworth's (white) stick during a final round grade match in Perth. Brian Glencross moves in to support team mate Walsh. Terry has placed his stick in such a position as to prevent Richard from playing the ball. Terry would be penalised for stick obstruction.

In photograph 4 observe how Richard has played the ball around Brian and attempts to retrieve it. Photograph 5 shows Brian turning and placing his body between Richard and the ball. In doing so he has clearly obstructed Richard from playing the ball.

4

5

3 Body contact

Players are not permitted to in any way push, shove or make contact with an opponent or the opponent's stick. A player's stick is also not to be used in a fashion which intimidates the opponent or hits the ball in a manner which is dangerous to other players. Hockey is a non-contact sport and such occurrences as shown in photograph 6 should be avoided by young players. In photograph 6 Australian vice-captain Jim Irvine is tackling Indian centre forward Grewal Singh during the 1979 World Tournament in Perth. Jim is clearly using his body to the disadvantage of his opponent and deserves to be penalised.

6

4 The stick

Only the flat side of the stick may be used by a player. Any other portion of the stick used will bring a penalty. A player's stick must never be raised above the shoulder.

5 Ball striking body

No player may use any part of the body to play the ball (except of course the goalkeeper). The hand may be used to catch the ball on the condition that the hand is stationary and the ball is dropped immediately to be played with the stick (see chapter on general skills).

Awarding penalties

Umpires can penalise players for breaching the rules by giving a free hit to the team which has been offended by that breach. Where the breach occurs inside the offending team's defensive circle a penalty corner will be given. Young players should also note that deliberate breaches inside the defensive 25 yard (22.7 metre) line can also result in a penalty corner.

Where the umpire believes an intentional breach has occurred within the circle by a defender a penalty stroke may be awarded. This penalty can also be awarded if the breach is unintentional but directly prevents a goal being scored.

For details of these set plays — penalty corners and penalty strokes — see the chapter devoted to set plays.

Unfair or unduly rough play

Where a player consistently offends the rules in a clearly unfair manner an umpire may stop the game and warn the offender for his or her misconduct. If it continues the umpire may temporarily suspend a player or even expel him or her from the game altogether.

Young players should never allow themselves to get into a situation such as this. As mentioned at the beginning of this chapter, players should respect the rules of the game and not bring it into disrepute by bad behaviour.

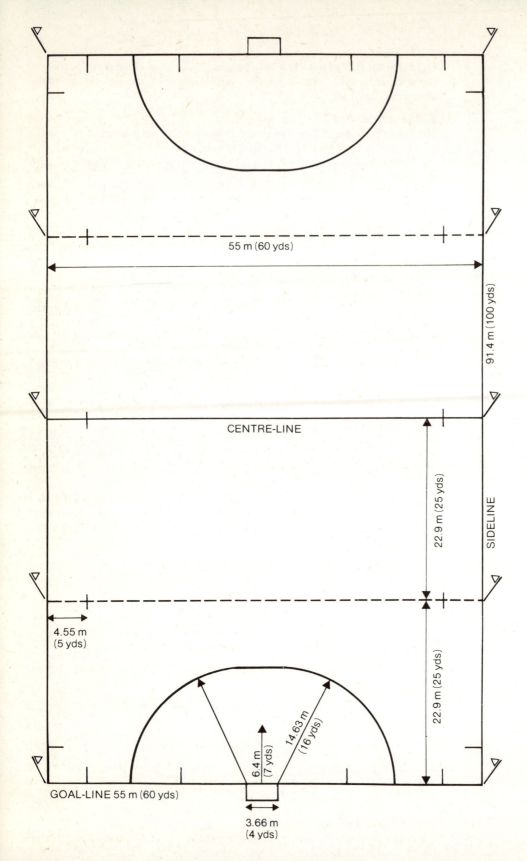

55 m (60 yds)

91.4 m (100 yds)

CENTRE-LINE

22.9 m (25 yds)

SIDELINE

22.9 m (25 yds)

4.55 m
(5 yds)

14.63 m
(16 yds)

6.4 m
(7 yds)

GOAL-LINE 55 m (60 yds)

3.66 m
(4 yds)

12 Coaching the young hockey player

Coaching a young hockey player is no easy assignment. In this book it is a stated aim to provide a basis of fundamental ideas which young hockey players can use to prepare for their future in the game. Every coach obviously stresses the need to learn basic skills such as those outlined in these pages. However, with teenage players who are normally drawn together in a competitive situation, a coach finds that the need to win tends to alter the ideal learning environment.

For a beginning player a coach of course must present hockey in a fun way. No early pressure to succeed in a competitive sense should be placed on the new player. In contemporary hockey this usually applies to those people younger than teenage who ideally are brought up with a modified approach to the game. Various systems of modified hockey have proven very successful in introducing the very basic ideas of hockey.

Once the foundations have been laid and a pleasurable and positive attitude has been gained the young hockey player moves into a team and match situation. Now the need to win becomes difficult to harness in a positive sense. Even at junior level there is pressure on coaches to produce competitively successful teams. This probably filters down from top sporting levels where a coach is too often held responsible for a team's success or lack of success. The pressure to win forces a coach to make too many decisions too early in a player's development. How many times do the following situations occur?

> The biggest and quite often best player placed at centre half and left there whether suitable for the position or not. By virtue of physical capabilities the early developer can often dominate a game and heavily influence its outcome.

> The best player placed at inside forward but rarely at wing or wing half.

> The beginner put to left wing and left there.

> The big hitter put to either fullback position.

> The least co-ordinated and least mobile player placed as goalkeeper — illogical, as a goalkeeper can virtually win or lose any match.

Regardless of the competitive nature of his team a coach should consider these thoughts:

> Rotation of players in positions on a reasonably regular basis would help to produce more flexible well rounded players.

> Should we not have forwards who have a defender's ability to time a tackle?

> Should we not have a defender whose knowledge of forward play enables the anticipation of a forward's likely moves?

The coach and the club
A coach is often hamstrung by the desires of his club, parents, supporters

and players, to win. And of course we must all be aiming to win in any competitive situation. Otherwise why bother to compete? But why can't a coach at this and any level be judged by different criteria? A club should establish guidelines for its junior coaches on these lines:

How well does the coach organise training?

Is there an atmosphere of rapport and harmony amongst team members which has been fostered by the coach?

Do the players respect the coach and play in an accordingly disciplined style?

Does the coach correct faults in play in a positive constructive manner?

Does the coach take time out to explain to his or her players exactly what is required of them? See photograph 1 as West Australian women's coach David Hatt discusses tactics with several of his players.

Do the players enjoy playing hockey?

A good junior coach may not have taught his side to win at age 15. That side may have learnt the basics of the game but be physically inferior to opponents, and consequently be harshly judged. A destructive junior coach may have been harmful to the long-term future of his players, yet be a consistent winner.

The coach's reaction to a loss is most important to a junior hockey team. Point out weaknesses by all means but endeavour not to dampen enthusiasm by unduly harsh criticism. A team of youngsters looks to its coach for the proper way to accept a defeat.

1

What should a junior coach do?

Some things a coach should be wary of have been outlined, but what are some other factors which should be taken into consideration before taking charge of the junior squad? Perhaps these things are relevant:

Have a realistic level of expectation of the rate of skill acquisition of the young player.

Make allowances for differing stages of physical and emotional maturity.

Allow for the fact that juniors show a relatively high level of inconsistency in training and match situations.

Avoid making premature and inflexible decisions on players' suitabilities for positions. Most players will not object to change. How else does one really understand the frustration of a winger who is not receiving a share of passes?

Treating the individual

Encourage the skilful player to use a natural talent to beat opponents during a game. Why ask players to dribble around objects at training and then chastise them for putting it into practice in matches?

Encourage team play by quick accurate passing but allow forwards in particular to take on a defender. An opponent who is in two minds about what a player may do with the ball is always easier to beat than one who is confident about what will happen when his opponent does just one thing all the time.

Foster the individual's desire to score goals. Don't ask the player to pass when in a scoring position. Avoid the continual habit of trying to force a penalty corner. Permit a player with natural scoring talent to practise and use that skill in a match.

Praising the young player

Like any other sportsman, the young hockey player reacts to praise and constructive criticism.

Do correct faults during training or in match situations in a thoughtful, positive way.

Don't aimlessly rant and rave at a youngster. This merely provides a fear of failure or a negative attitude to the game.

Functions which are performed well should be praised at the time they occur and reinforced later.

Don't forget to praise things which are less obvious than say goal scoring or the continuous winning of possession, for example:
1   The player who runs hard to be in position to accept a pass which is not given.
2   The player who thinks to "cover defend" when a dangerous situation looks like developing.
3   Position play which results in opposing players being restricted in their opportunities.
4   The player who vocally encourages his team mates throughout a game.

5   The players who have directly contributed in the scoring of a goal, other than the goal scorer who will be praised anyway.

6   Attempts to put into practice things which have been done in training, whether they have been ultimately successful or not.

Approach to training

Above all else the coach must be *organised*. Carefully prepare each session with the team members. Keep the following things in mind when carrying out a training session:

Make each session enjoyable. Young people should want to train for hockey.

Vary the skills exercises and don't allow any particular one to drag on for too long.

Be clear and concise in instructions given to players. Don't talk for long periods.

Be encouraging and obviously enthusiastic about the game.

Set the example about punctuality before training and match situations.

When demonstration is required be able to execute it yourself or have someone who can do it for you.

Be firm with players who deliberately or continually upset team discipline.

Isolate match faults and eradicate them at training. Note in photographs 2, 3 and 4 how David Hatt takes time to correct individual faults during a training session or demonstrates where necessary.

The match

Just as careful thought goes into planning a training session, the coach should not confront match days without planning the warm-up his team should be doing, and what should be said in the pre-match address.

The talk before a game should not be a fire and brimstone collection of melodramatic urgings for grand victory. Rather it should be a measured summary of the efforts needed from each player and a concise outline of their individual responsibilities. Motivation is obviously necessary, but it should be approached from the point of view of the mastery of the skills of the game, and through that the mastery of opponents.

During the game the coaching can positively reinforce the approach taken to that particular match and at half-time offer praise and appropriate criticism. The after-game summary should be of the same nature. Those things poorly done can be discussed and solutions offered. Those things well done can be highlighted. Always try to leave the young player in a positive frame of mind.

A suggested training session

It is to be stressed that this training session is merely a suggested format and by no means to be taken as appropriate for all teams and conditions.

A basic premise of this outline is that it is of more value to train well for a relatively short time, than to spend long periods where boredom and inactivity may become evident.

1 Warm-up and stretching exercises (5-10 minutes)
This initial section can include a set period of running (at various speeds)

2

3

4

interspersed with or preceded by stretching and agility exercises which are directed towards:

- Calf muscles

- Hamstring muscles

- Thigh muscles

- Arm and shoulder muscles

- Wrist

- Lower back

The object should be to warm up muscles by increasing the blood flow to these muscle groups. Stretching can also be undertaken before the initial run is begun.

A useful principle to be followed is that all such exercises be done with a slow beginning with gradually increased stress. There is much literature available on this aspect and a wide variety of movements can be employed.

Exercises can be done in pairs. See photographs 5, 6 and 7 for examples of the types of stretching exercises which can be done.

5

6

7

2 Ball skills

- Balance ball on stick after bouncing ball on stick as few times as possible.

- Bounce ball on stick as many times as possible in a specific time period.

- Using the same principles, players in pairs should pass the ball between each other without letting the ball touch the ground.

- Jogging with the ball up and down the field.

- Continue jogging with ball, but in and out of obstacles, changing speed and direction at random.

- Repeat at greater speeds.

- Pushing and trapping at speed from close range.

3 Skills practices (20-25 minutes)

Select any one or two skills areas and concentrate on these. (For suggested practices see earlier chapters.) Perhaps a particular skill which has been poorly performed in a previous game can be selected.

Note suggested exercises in photograph 8 where the women demonstrate hitting and trapping in pairs and in photograph 9 where the men are involved in a tackling and dribbling exercise.

8

9

Finish the skills session with an exercise such as the one shown below which involves all your team in continuous movement.

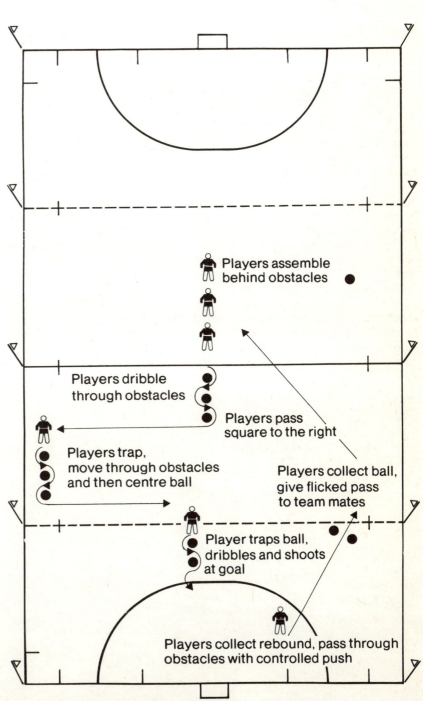

Players assemble behind obstacles

Players dribble through obstacles

Players pass square to the right

Players trap, move through obstacles and then centre ball

Players collect ball, give flicked pass to team mates

Player traps ball, dribbles and shoots at goal

Players collect rebound, pass through obstacles with controlled push

Suggested team practice involving most skills

4 Simulated game skills practices (10-15 minutes)

To simulate the game situation and make it enjoyable almost any idea can be used. Assuming a squad of 12 players, half the field can be used to play six against six with the goalkeeper on one team. Rules for such a game are adaptable. For example, if you wish to emphasise the push pass then hitting can be banned. Other variations may include:

- Five consecutive passes without interception equals one goal.

- Three good tackles for possession equals one goal.

- One team holding possession for thirty seconds or more equals one goal.

- Reduce the size of the playing area to one quarter of the field.

To develop understanding between players and increase the degree of participation decrease the size of teams to two against two. The resulting continuous action is also good for developing stamina.

5 Set plays (15-20 minutes)

Depending on what is seen as necessary by the coach, a good proportion of most training sessions can be spent on set plays. For example, the whole team can be occupied in practising offensive and defensive penalty corners and corners. The chapter in this book dealing with set plays should be particularly helpful when considering what can be done in this area. It is important that things like penalty strokes, push-ins and free hits in important positions are not neglected in sessions such as these.

This suggested session would normally occupy just over 60 minutes of continued activity. After allowing for further time for instruction, demonstration or explanation in normal circumstances this is the optimum period for beginning hockey players.

Fitness is gained by the efforts given to skills practice. Young players should have a reasonable degree of natural fitness, but attention can be given to the skill of running as speed is a very important factor in modern hockey. Correct running *technique* should be taught at an early age. This is particularly so if the young player has interstate or international aspirations.

13 Preparation for the match

Every young hockey player should have a basic intention in playing in any hockey match. The aim should be to enjoy the game by gaining pleasure from a wholehearted individual effort which helps the team to play to the fullest extent of its ability. To fulfil this aim many things must be done by a hockey player.

Mental preparation

Even at the early stages in a hockey playing career care should be taken to prepare mentally for a game. In the time leading up to a fixture ask some of the following questions of yourself:

Have I a positive attitude to the game? My first thoughts should be to relax and enjoy the prospect of a game of hockey.

What are the positional responsibilities I may have, and what is their order of importance?

How can I best help my team mates?

What are the things my coach has asked me to concentrate on?

In what condition is the surface on which the match is to be played?

What weaknesses were evident in my last match which I can hope to overcome during this match?

Which strengths did I have in my last match which I can continue to show?

Thinking along these lines will help your concentration during the match itself. If you have some problems why not talk them over with your team mates after training? The ability to think through situations which may occur, picture yourself dealing with them and creating play yourself is the first step in actually being able to carry out ideas *on the field*.

Playing gear and equipment

All successful hockey players take great care that they have correctly dressed themselves for a match. They have also made sure their extra equipment is in order for the game. The best way to be consistent in this important area is to make yourself a checklist which you can go through when getting ready for a match. Perhaps this list provides a useful guideline:

Socks, skirt/shorts, shirt

Boots or shoes appropriate for surface

Shin pads

Garters

Mouth guard

Head band (if worn)

Track suit or warm-up suit

Wet gear if conditions require it

Spare boot laces

Hockey stick(s)

Roll of adhesive tape for stick or boot repairs.

1

This list covers every contingency and if adhered to assures that you will never be the one trying to borrow someone else's equipment at the last minute. *Note:* The importance of shin pads and mouth guard cannot be too firmly expressed. These are vital for protection from serious injury.

In photograph 1 note how Australian international player Craig Davies takes the trouble to carefully adjust his shin pads and has not forgotten his mouth guard.

Warm-up for the game

Be punctual for the game, allowing plenty of time for your warm-up. Your coach or manager will usually require you to be at the ground by a certain time. Once there you should establish a normal routine of exercises. Some have been suggested in the warm-up section of the suggested training session earlier in this book.

Basically, before doing anything a light jog and warm-up exercises (in a slow, leisurely fashion) should be undertaken. Remember also to pay attention to your arms and back. If you are to be a successful player your back must be bent and to ignore this area is to invite trouble in your future playing career. Many players make the error of paying attention only to their legs. While the leg muscles must be warmed up and stretched methodically (first calves then quadriceps and hamstrings) it is essential that the arms and upper body and back are also included in the warm-up. Circling exercises with the arms both anti-clockwise and clockwise are very useful, as are various passive stretches. The neck and back are vital to any hockey player and should be carefully looked after. Gentle rotation (in both directions) and flexion and extension of the neck should suffice. To increase back flexibility "touching the toes" is not recommended as it can do more harm than good. It is better to lie on your back and start with gentle sit-up exercises, gradually increasing. Then, lift the bent knees onto the stomach then shoulders and eventually if you are able, touch straight legs on the ground behind your head! If you are able to eventually develop this degree of flexibility you will probably have few back problems.

Note in photographs 2 and 3 how Australian player Dianne Walsh executes some of her warm-up activities. Dianne is a superb athlete with a most professional approach.

Once your body has been prepared, move to a series of skills practices which can be followed by more explosive running and skills execution.

If your coach allows you a certain time to yourself you can consider the following options:

1   Practise your set plays — short corners, penalty strokes etc.

2   Practise all the basic skills for a short period each — especially short sharp activities such as tackling and pushing and stopping over a short distance.

2

3

3   Join the team immediately prior to the match for short sharp sprints to get yourself in tune for a quick start to the game.

   You should now be in a state of sound mental and physical preparation for your match.

OTHER TITLES IN
THE YOUNG SPORTSMAN SERIES

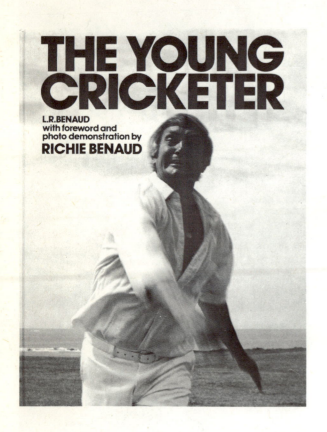

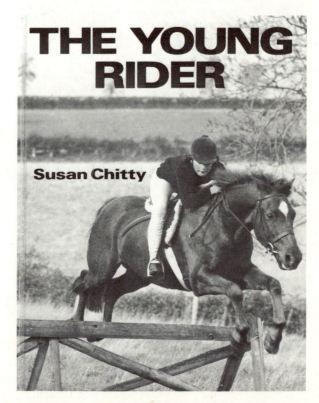

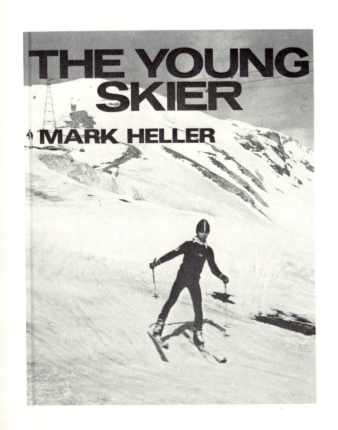

THE YOUNG
SKIER
MARK HELLER

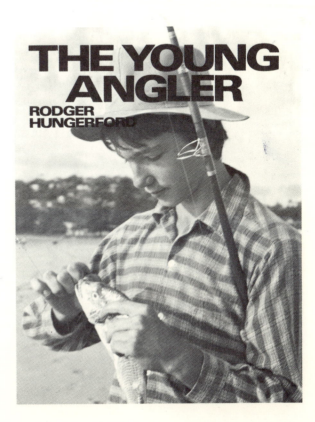

THE YOUNG
ANGLER
RODGER
HUNGERFORD